The education and employment of disabled young people

The education and employment of disabled young people

Frustrated ambition

Tania Burchardt

JOSEPH ROWNTREE
FOUNDATION

First published in Great Britain in November 2005 by

The Policy Press
Fourth Floor, Beacon House
Queen's Road
Bristol BS8 1QU
UK

Tel no +44 (0)117 331 4054
Fax no +44 (0)117 331 4093
Email   tpp-info@bristol.ac.uk
www.policypress.org.uk

Published for the Joseph Rowntree Foundation by The Policy Press

ISBN 1 86134 807 X

British Library Cataloguing in Publication Data
A catalogue record for this book is available from the British Library.

Library of Congress Cataloging-in-Publication Data
A catalog record for this book has been requested.

Tania Burchardt is a senior research fellow at the London School of Economics and Political Science.

The **Joseph Rowntree Foundation** has supported this project as part of its programme of research and innovative development projects, which it hopes will be of value to policy makers, practitioners and service users. The facts presented and views expressed in this report are, however, those of the author and not necessarily those of the Foundation.

The statements and opinions contained within this publication are solely those of the author and not of The University of Bristol or The Policy Press. The University of Bristol and The Policy Press disclaim responsibility for any injury to persons or property resulting from any material published in this publication.

The Policy Press works to counter discrimination on grounds of gender, race, disability, age and sexuality.

Cover design by Qube Design Associates, Bristol
Printed in Great Britain by Hobbs the Printers Ltd, Southampton

Contents

List of tables, figures and boxes

Tables

Figures

Boxes

Acknowledgements

This report is the result of research funded by the Joseph Rowntree Foundation (JRF), to whom I am very grateful. Specifically, I am grateful to the support of Mark Hinman and Chris Goulden who guided the project on behalf of the Foundation. I would also like to thank the seven young people who agreed to be interviewed for this study and who were generous and candid in sharing their thoughts and experiences with me. I am grateful to Skill, London Connexions and the Tower Project for helping to put me in touch with potential interviewees. I benefited throughout the project from an advisory group: Ann Gross, Jenny Morris, David Piachaud, Ingrid Schoon, Louca-Mai Wilson and Kevin Woods. My thanks to them for giving freely of their time and for their constructive criticism. Laura Lane helped me proficiently with data coding; Tanvi Desai, Jane Dickson, Lucy Himeur, Gordon Knowles, Irina Verkhova and Nic Warner provided their usual cheerful and efficient computing and admin support. Survey data were made available via the Centre for Longitudinal Studies at the Institute for Education and the Data Archive at the University of Essex. Responsibility for the interpretation of the data, and any errors of fact or judgement, remains mine alone.

Summary

Background

This report is about the transitions young people make from compulsory education to early adult life, comparing the experiences of disabled and non-disabled young people. It explores the aspirations young people develop for further education and future employment, and the extent to which those aspirations are achieved. Aside from their instrumental importance in securing good educational and occupational outcomes, positive aspirations for the future – and being able to make choices in pursuit of them – are important aspects of autonomy.

Disabled young people have not always been encouraged to see themselves as having a valuable role to play in adult society. Previous research on a sample of young people born in 1958 reported that the proportion of disabled youngsters who aspired to semi-skilled and unskilled jobs was six times the proportion of non-disabled young people with those aspirations (Walker, 1982). Despite these modest aspirations, only one fifth of disabled 18-year-olds had achieved the occupational group of the job they had desired at age 16, compared to one third of non-disabled youngsters, and the gap between aspirations and outcomes for disabled young people was wider than the gap for non-disabled young people.

This report asks whether the gap between disabled and non-disabled young people's aspirations, and the even larger gap in their subsequent attainment, has remained the same for groups of young people born more recently. It uses two main sources of data:

- the 1970 British Cohort Study (BCS70);
- the Youth Cohort Studies (YCS).

The BCS70 provides detailed information at ages 16 and 26 about young people born in 1970. The YCS provide less detailed but more up-to-date information about young people at ages 16-19. The groups examined here were born in 1982-85.

Policy frameworks

There has been a tendency for disabled young people to be considered as disabled first and children afterwards, rather than the other way round, but the strategy document, *Every child matters* (DfES, 2003), is explicitly universal in scope. Among other objectives, it highlights the importance of enabling young people to make a positive contribution and to achieve economic well-being. Both of these are crucial in supporting the transition of disabled young people to adulthood. At the same time, the Cabinet Office (2005) report, *Improving the life chances of disabled people*, highlighted transition to adulthood and employment as key areas for improvement. With these over-arching frameworks in place, the stage is set for significant progress to be made.

Complexity of transition

The account below is a real case study drawn from the BCS70 data and all the information is as reported by, or about, the young person (the name is fictional, of course). A fuller version is provided in the main report but even this abbreviated account illustrates the range of influences potentially operating on a young person.

Dan's story

Dan is an only child, who at age 16 is living with his mother. She left school at the earliest opportunity but is now studying part time. Dan's father, who was educated to degree level, died when Dan was 10. The family income is very low – under £50 per week. Dan has a sight impairment, which the school nurse considers results in 'some interference' with his daily life.

He attends mainstream school and has a generally positive attitude to school and school work, although he has often felt anxious or depressed in the last year.

Dan wants to go on to higher education. (His mother also hopes and expects him to stay on in education.) His ideal job would be a bank manager.

He is highly motivated and a firm believer in his ability to control his own fate. He feels he has little support from his mother and wants to leave home now or very soon.

******

By age 26, Dan is part way through a professional accounting qualification, having achieved eight 'O' levels, two CSE grade 1s, four A levels and a degree.

He works full time as an accounts clerk in a large firm and has never been unemployed since leaving college. He earns £208 per week take home pay (just slightly above the average for all employees in the sample).

He is cohabiting with his girlfriend in a house they are buying with a mortgage.

In many ways, Dan's is a success story. As illustrated in the main report, however, not everyone's account has such a happy ending. Each individual's circumstances are unique and the range and interplay between different factors is highly complex. The process is anything but deterministic.

The figure opposite shows the framework used for analysis.

Figure 1.1: Framework for analysis

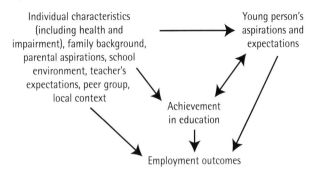

Aspirations

The scope and level of aspirations of disabled and non-disabled 16-year-olds were found to be similar:

- 62% of disabled young people wanted to stay on after 16, compared to 60% of non-disabled young people (source: BCS70 age 16);
- 33% of disabled young people aspired to a professional occupation, compared to 24% of non-disabled young people (source: BCS70 age 16);
- the average weekly pay disabled and non-disabled 16/17-year-olds expected to get from a full-time job was similar (source: YCS age 16/17).

Some groups among the disabled population did seem to be at risk of lower aspirations, although the sub-samples were too small for differences to be statistically robust:

- young people with mental health problems;
- those with more severe impairments or more complex needs;
- those who became disabled later in childhood.

For all young people, there is a strong gradient in educational and occupational aspirations with respect to their parents' educational and social class background. Young people who have parents neither of whom have any educational qualifications are more than four times as likely to intend to leave education at 16 than young people who have at least one parent educated to degree level.

Aside from external influences, the young person's own motivation and outlook is also crucial. This appears to be especially the case for disabled young people: those with a firmer belief in their ability to shape their future are more likely to aim high.

Educational outcomes

At age 16/17,

- 71% of non-disabled respondents were in full-time education, compared to 62% of disabled respondents (source: YCS age 16/17);
- three fifths of non-disabled people report that they got the education or training place, or job, that they wanted, while only just over half of disabled youngsters say the same (source: YCS age 16/17).

By age 18/19,

- the highest qualification of 48% of disabled young people is at NVQ level 1 or below (including those with no qualifications), compared to 28% of non-disabled young people (source: YCS age 18/19).
- disabled young people still in education at this age are more likely than their non-disabled peers to be pursuing secondary-level or vocational qualifications (source: YCS age 18/19).

At age 26,

- the educational attainment of two fifths (41%) of young people who were disabled at both age 16 and age 26 fell below their initial level of aspiration, compared to 35% of young people who were disabled at neither age (source: BCS70 age 16 and 26).

Multivariate analysis showed that educational aspirations are an important, independent, influence on educational outcomes, for disabled and non-disabled young people alike. The previous section found that the aspirations of disabled and non-disabled young people were similar. However, controlling for other characteristics such as parental education, young people who become disabled between the ages of 16 and 26, and those who are disabled at both ages, have lower educational attainment *relative to their aspirations* than do their non-disabled counterparts.

Occupational outcomes

The gap between the proportion of disabled and non-disabled people out of work widens as they get older:

- at age 16/17, disabled young people are about twice as likely as non-disabled young people to be out of work or 'doing something else' (13% compared to 7%) (source: YCS age 16/17);
- by age 18/19, disabled young people were nearly three times as likely as non-disabled adults of the same age to be unemployed or 'doing something else' (25% compared to 9%) (source: YCS age 18/19);
- at age 26, young people who were disabled at age 16 and at age 26 were nearly four times as likely to be unemployed or 'sick/disabled' than young people who were disabled at neither age (13.8% compared to 3.7%) (source: BCS70 age 26. Note that this is an earlier cohort than the YCS, so not strictly comparable).

Among those who were in employment, earnings were lower for disabled than for non-disabled employees, both at age 18/19 (in the YCS cohorts) and at age 26 (in the BCS70 cohort). At age 26, disabled young people were earning 11% less than their non-disabled counterparts with the same educational qualifications.

Occupational outcomes fell below aspirations for many young people, but the gap was larger for disabled young people than for non-disabled young people: 39% of young people disabled at both ages fell below their initial aspiration level, compared to 28% of non-disabled young people.

Frustrated ambition

The encouraging aspect of these results is that the aspirations of disabled and non-disabled teenagers appear to have converged since the 1970s. The large gaps in the aspirations of disabled and non-disabled 16-year-olds found in earlier research on a cohort of young people who were aged 16 in 1974 (Walker, 1982), were not replicated among the cohorts studied in this research, who were aged 16 in 1986 and in 1998/ 2000 respectively. The raising of disabled young people's aspirations is surely to be welcomed.

The discouraging aspect is that disabled people's experience of early adult life continues to be beset by frustration and disappointment; high aspirations are not translated into comparable educational or occupational attainment. This is reflected in a widening gap between the disabled and non-disabled young people in various measures of confidence and subjective well-being: by age 26, disabled young people are less confident of the strengths they bring to the labour market, have a higher malaise score and are three times more likely to agree that 'Whatever I do has no real effect on what happens to me', while at age 16 there was no significant difference between them and their non-disabled peers on any of these measures.

Better targeted advice and encouragement to form positive educational and occupational aspirations may be required for some specific groups among disabled teenagers: those with mental health problems, more complex needs, or who become disabled later in childhood, were identified above as being at risk of low aspirations. In addition, this study has not looked at those with learning difficulties, many of whom may need encouragement to formulate their own independent aspirations.

However the main effort must focus on transforming the actual opportunities available to disabled young people, for example:

- The transition from school to further education remains problematic. Continuity of support, including funding, equipment and personnel, may be an important part of the solution.
- Programmes such as New Deal for Disabled People and Pathways to Work, which are designed to provide incentives and advice for disabled people to move into employment, are misdirected for disabled young people, since motivation is not lacking among this group. Work placements, combined with extending the availability of Access to Work to cover work experience, might prove to be a more effective approach.
- Serious attention must be given to the question of equal pay, and to the *widening* gaps between disabled and non-disabled young people's participation in employment as they move into early adulthood.

It has been a struggle for young disabled people to gain recognition of their potential and to develop positive aspirations for playing useful roles in adult life. That achievement is certainly to be celebrated. But the fact that equality of opportunity in turning those aspirations into reality is still far from realised leaves no room for complacency.

Introduction

Motivation

This report is about the transitions young people make from compulsory education to early adult life. There have been several research programmes and numerous individual projects on this topic, so it is legitimate to ask what is distinctive about this research. The answer is two-fold:

- it focuses on the experiences of disabled young people, in comparison to their non-disabled peers;
- it explores the aspirations young people develop for further education and future employment, and the extent to which those aspirations are achieved.

Many studies of disabled young people making the transition to adult life have shed light on the barriers to achieving independent living, the sometimes far from smooth transfer from 'children' to 'adult' social services, and relationships with parents and friends (for example, Morris, 1999a; Hendey and Pascall, 2001; Morris, 2002; Dean 2003). These are all important issues. But if social inclusion is the overall objective, gaining skills and qualifications, and taking one's first steps in the labour market are also crucial. Less is known about the transitions disabled young people make in these respects; a gap this study contributes to filling.

Research on young people in general has shown that aspirations can play a key role in the achievement of educational qualifications and subsequent occupational outcomes. Studies on several cohorts of young people[1] over the last few decades have found that having high aspirations is associated with better employment outcomes in early adulthood, independently of other characteristics such as parental background or schooling (for example, Maziels, 1970; O'Brien and Jones, 1999; Schoon, 2001). Avoiding unemployment in early adulthood is particularly important because unemployment at this stage in the career has a 'scarring effect' on later employment prospects (Gregg, 2001).

Aside from their instrumental importance in securing good educational and occupational outcomes, positive aspirations for the future – and being able to make choices in pursuit of them – are important aspects of autonomy. Disabled young people have not always been encouraged to see themselves as having a valuable role to play in adult society and this may have translated into unduly limited aspirations (Preece, 1996; Mitchell, 1999; Wilson, 2003). Examining the formation of educational and employment aspirations, and the prospects for translating those aspirations into reality, is therefore an important part of assessing the degree of autonomy that young disabled people are afforded in our society.

Research questions

The questions this report seeks to answer are:

(1) We know that disabled young people are less likely to gain educational qualifications than non-disabled young people. To what extent is this due to (i) their parental background, (ii) their own low aspirations or others' aspirations for them, or (iii) something else? Of course the answer may well turn out to be a mixture of these three. Included in the catch-all third category is the possibility that disabled young people are less well-served by the education system or that they face direct discrimination.

---

[1] A group of people born in the same year or period is referred to as a 'cohort'. In the remainder of the report, I will sometimes use that terminology, for example, to compare the '1958 cohort' with the '1970 cohort'.

(2) We also know that disabled young people spend more time out of work and that those who do secure employment are disproportionately found in low-skilled, low-status occupations, compared to their non-disabled peers. To what extent is this due to (i) their educational qualifications, (ii) other background characteristics, (iii) low occupational aspirations, or (iv) something else?

(3) Previous research on a sample of young people born in 1958 reported that the gap between aspirations and outcomes for disabled young people was wider than the gap for non-disabled young people. Has this remained the case for groups of young people born more recently?

Scope of research

This report focuses on comparing non-disabled young people with young people with physical or sensory impairments, and those with mental health problems. Young people with learning difficulties (sometimes called intellectual or cognitive impairment) are not included in either the disabled or the non-disabled group for the purposes of this study. According to the social model of disability, it is important to distinguish between disadvantage that arises directly from the nature of the impairment and disadvantage that arises from the circumstances in which people with impairments find themselves. Cognitive impairment is likely to have a direct effect on the attainment of qualifications and subsequent labour market experience. By contrast, there is no reason to expect that young people with physical or sensory impairments, or mental health problems, have less academic or labour market potential, on average, than their non-disabled peers. Any difference in achievement can therefore be attributed to circumstances rather than to the intrinsic effects of impairment. Accordingly, wherever possible, the results use a classification of disability status excluding young people with learning difficulties. Of course, this is not to imply that the experiences and achievements of young people with learning difficulties are less important or worthy of analysis, it is simply that they are not the subject of this study.

Many studies on education use classifications based on special educational needs (SEN). There

is overlap between children with SEN and disabled children but they are not identical populations. On the one hand, some disabled children do not need any additional help to access the curriculum, and some would benefit from help but their need is not identified. On the other hand, many children with SEN have emotional and behavioural problems that are not associated with an impairment or with a recognised mental illness. The definitions of both SEN and disability are far from clear cut and in practice the 'label' an individual young person has in the data we use for analysis is determined by judgements made in particular cases by professionals, researchers, and – sometimes – by the young person themselves.

Young people who attended special schools are included in the research[2] but they make up too small a proportion of the population to be able to analyse their circumstances separately within the general purpose surveys that this research uses.

Methods and data

The research began with seven in-depth interviews with disabled people aged 17 to 24, which were used to orientate the researcher to the issues that young people themselves felt had been important in shaping their aspirations, their experience of education, and any experience they had of employment. The young people were contacted through a range of disability organisations. Their circumstances varied from a graduate, living independently and in full-time employment, to a young woman studying for GCSEs at a further education college and living with her mother. The interviewees came from a range of ethnic and socioeconomic backgrounds, and their impairments included spastic quadriplegia, cerebral palsy, ME, asthma, visual impairment and deafness.[3] Accounts of these interviews are not given directly but the themes that emerged are reported where relevant. Insights gained from the interviews were used to

---

[2] Except in analysis using the YCS, which excludes pupils at special school at age 16.

[3] None of the interviewees reported mental health problems. It would have been valuable to include the perspectives of young people with mental health problems in this part of the study. However, they are included in the quantitative analysis.

Box 1.1: 1970 British Cohort Study (BCS70)

- All children born in Britain in a particular week in 1970.
- Surveys at birth, age 5, 10, 16 (in 1986), 26 (in 1996) and 30.
- At age 16, information collected from the young person themselves, parents, school, and a medical examination.
- At age 26, information collected only from the respondent.
- Funded by a range of government departments and charitable trusts. Now run by the Centre for Longitudinal Studies at the Institute of Education.

Sample sizes
- At birth: 16,135 babies = 98% response rate.
- At age 16, difficulties of tracing and data collection were compounded by industrial action being taken by teachers. At least one part of the survey was completed by (or about) 11,628 members of the original sample = 72% response rate.
- At age 26, 9,003 completed a postal questionnaire = 56% of original sample.

Attrition bias
Fortunately, several researchers have investigated the possible bias arising from respondents dropping out of the survey (attrition) (see Despotidou and Shepherd, 2002). Even at age 26, the achieved sample is fairly similar in composition to previous sweeps. However, those who have previously reported a health problem or impairment are slightly under-represented; as are young people from a
minority ethnic background, who were born to a single mother, unemployed father or a parent from a lower social class background; those with low school achievement; those who grew up in families with financial problems; and those who have experienced poor housing conditions. Where possible, these characteristics are controlled for in multivariate analysis.

inform the subsequent data analysis and interpretation.

The main part of the research uses two large-scale, nationally representative surveys. The first is the 1970 British Cohort Study (BCS70), details of which are given in Box 1.1. The main advantages of the BCS70 are the richness of its data and the fact that we have information about the same young people at age 16, at a time when they are making critical decisions about their future, and at age 26, when most have completed formal education and have made their first forays into the labour market. The main drawback of the survey for the purposes of this research is that the young people reached the age of 16 in 1986, a period rather different from the present in terms of both the economic and policy context.[4]

In order to provide a more contemporary picture, data from the BCS70 are complemented with analysis of the Youth Cohort Studies (YCS), described in Box 1.2. Although the period for which we observe these young people is shorter, from age 16 to age 18 or 19, their experience is of the current education system and labour market. Combining two cohorts from the YCS gives a large sample size and the surveys contain detailed information about qualifications and employment. However, the information about family background, and about disability, is more limited than in the BCS70.

In the BCS70, young people are identified as disabled at age 16 using a combination of information from parents and health professionals, and at age 26 from the young person themselves. In the YCS, young people are identified as disabled by their response to a question approximating the 1995 Disability Discrimination Act definition of disability. Further details of the questions used to identify disabled young people in the two surveys are given in the Appendix.

Framework for analysis

Figure 1.1 presents a simplified framework for understanding the relationship between a range

---

[4] Of course, if one wants to observe what happens to people in their mid-twenties, their teenage years will necessarily be some time in the past.

Box 1.2: Youth Cohort Studies (YCS)

- New cohort of 16/17-year-olds in England and Wales every two years.
- Includes state and private school pupils but excludes special schools, pupil referral units and schools with less than 20 Year 11 pupils.
- Cohort 9, born 1982/83, surveyed at age 16/17 (in 1998), 17/18 and 18/19 (sweeps 1 to 3).
- Cohort 10, born 1984/85, surveyed at age 16/17 (in 2000, twice), and 18/19 (sweeps 1 to 3).
- Primarily postal questionnaire, plus some telephone interviews.
- Funded and run by the Department for Education and Skills.

Sample sizes
- Cohort 9, sweep 1: 14,761 (= 66% response rate)
- Cohort 9, sweep 3: 6,304 (= 65% of sweep 2, 43% of sweep 1)
- Cohort 10, sweep 1: 13,699 (= 55% response rate)
- Cohort 10, sweep 3: 7,247 (= 72% of sweep 2, 53% of sweep 1)

Weights calculated by the data providers to counteract non-response and attrition bias are used in the analysis where appropriate.

Figure 1.1: Framework for analysis

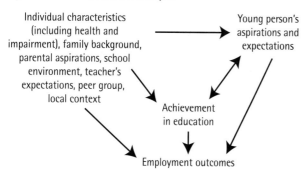

of factors and their impact on employment outcomes in early adult life. It illustrates the crucial mediating role of achievement in education, and the complex relationship with aspirations: both a cause and a result of educational achievement, and influencing employment outcomes both directly and indirectly. Impairment is shown in the top left corner as one among many personal characteristics that may affect aspirations, education and employment. Disability – the interaction between an individual's impairment and the physical, social and economic environment in which he or she operates – is represented by the contextual factors also listed in the top left corner.

The causal connections represented by the horizontal arrow will be investigated in Chapter 3. The relationships between aspirations and educational outcomes, and between background characteristics and educational outcomes, are described in chapter 4. Chapter 5 completes the analysis by looking at the influence of personal characteristics on occupational outcomes, mediated by education and aspirations.

Policy context

Children and young people have featured strongly in the Labour government's policies since coming to power in 1997. Whether as a result of the Prime Minister's early insistence that his top three priorities were 'education, education, education', or whether because an equal opportunity interpretation of social justice requires levelling the playing field between advantaged and disadvantaged children, the rate at which policy initiatives for young people have been announced has been brisk. Meanwhile, the employment situation of disabled adults has come under increasing scrutiny as welfare reform has rolled out across 'client groups' beyond those traditionally classed as unemployed. This section begins by describing two overarching policy frameworks before turning to more specific policy initiatives.

Frameworks

The current broad policy framework with respect to children was established by the government's Green Paper, *Every child matters*, published in 2003 (DfES, 2003). It set out proposals to reform the delivery of services that impact on children, including education, health, social services and the criminal justice system, and was followed in 2004 by the Children Act and a series of further documents giving more detailed guidance. The effectiveness of the new arrangements is to be assessed with respect to five outcomes, namely the extent to which children can:

- be healthy;
- stay safe;
- enjoy and achieve;
- make a positive contribution; and
- achieve economic well-being.

Enjoy and achieve includes "achieving stretching national educational standards"; *make a positive contribution* includes "developing self-confidence and successfully dealing with significant life changes and challenges"; and *achieve economic well-being* includes "engaging in further education, employment or training on leaving school", and being "ready for employment" (DfES, 2004a, Box 1). Moreover, the stated policy aim is to "improve those outcomes for all children and to narrow the gap in outcomes between those who do well and those who do not" (DfES, 2004a, p.4). The current study looks at a number of these outcomes, and examines one set of characteristics that often differentiates those who do well and those who do not, namely, disability.

A significant report on the long-term strategy for the social inclusion of disabled people, *Improving the life chances of disabled people* was published by the Cabinet Office in 2005. Realistically, although depressingly, it recognises that disabled people in Britain today are not "respected and included as equal members of society", and it sets the objective that by 2025, disabled people should have "full opportunities to improve their quality of life"(p 4).

Of particular relevance to this study, the Cabinet Office report identifies a smooth transition to adulthood, and support and incentives for getting and staying in employment, as two priority areas. With regard to transition, most of the recommendations concern social services and independent living rather than education and employment. With regard to employment, several of the recommendations focus on older disabled people, but the report does state that there is a need to improve the extent to which education

serves to provide disabled people with the skills employers want. It also notes the key role of employers, but sees this as being enhanced through advice and information rather than a more interventionist approach.

Curriculum reform

Overhauling the curriculum for 14- to 19-year-olds has been high on the policy agenda for a number of years. The Tomlinson report (Working Group on 14-19 Reform, 2004) identified the main problems as:

- too many young people leaving education lacking basic skills;
- fragmented vocational provision;
- excessive burden of assessment on pupils and teachers; and
- insufficient challenges offered for high attainers.

The working group also commented on the deterioration in motivation of young people as they moved up through the system. Although the Tomlinson report did not focus specifically on disabled young people, the first two of the issues identified are of particular relevance to disabled young people. Tomlinson recommended a unified diploma system, with each diploma including compulsory 'core' subjects such as maths, literacy, information technology and personal development, and an extended individual project, plus 'main learning' chosen by the pupil to reflect their interests and ambitions, selected from a range of vocational and academic courses.

The government has not adopted the recommendations of the Tomlinson report in full but it is supporting a modified version of the diplomas, and an emphasis on flexibility over where learning takes place and at what age different qualifications are obtained (DfES, 2005). For young people at risk of disengaging with education, a pilot programme for 14- to 16-year-olds is to be developed, using personal mentors and work-based courses, and leading to a new-style diploma. Critics argue that an opportunity to integrate vocational and academic study has been missed, with the danger that secondary education will become increasingly two-tier. This report explores whether disabled young people are disproportionately likely to be directed towards vocational rather than academic courses.

Special educational needs

In parallel with developments on the curriculum as a whole, the government produced a strategy for special educational needs (SEN) (DfES, 2004b), following two critical Audit Commission reports in 2002 (Audit Commission, 2002a, 2002b). The strategy acknowledges that, "All children have a right to a good education and the opportunity to fulfil their potential" (p 5), a right that has arguably not always been accessible to disabled children. To this end, teaching of children with SEN is to be given higher profile in teacher training courses, a framework of evidence-based teaching strategies for SEN is to be produced, and better tools for monitoring progress of pupils developed. School league tables will be revised to ensure that schools get credit for the attainment of children with SEN, rather than seeing them as a drain on average performance.

One of the four key areas identified as in need of attention is raising expectations – the expectations of the pupils themselves, their teachers, and their parents. The importance of the expectations of teachers and parents is a theme that recurs throughout this report too. The SEN strategy also commits the government to ensuring that young people with SEN are actively involved in decisions about their future post-16, and that they have opportunities for progression in education, training or employment.

The legislative framework for disabled pupils has developed in recent years. The SEN code of practice following the 1996 Education Act requires that planning for the post-16 transition of young people with SEN begins in year 9 (at age 14), with annual reviews subsequently. The 2001 SEN and Disability Act strengthens the rights of children with SEN to be educated in mainstream schools. In 2002, the part of the 1995 Disability Discrimination Act (DDA) that relates to educational institutions (part 4) came into force. This includes duties to make reasonable adjustments with respect to admissions policies, examinations and qualifications, and access to courses and resources, so that disabled pupils are not treated less favourably.

Research by the Disability Rights Commission indicated that these changes were sorely needed (Wilson, 2003). Its survey of disabled 16- to 24-year-olds found that 45% had experienced problems at school related to disability and 11% were unable to get access to resources such as the school library. One quarter had felt discriminated against due to their disability and over one third had been bullied. Between one in five and one in three said they had missed out on day trips or longer expeditions.

Further change is in the pipeline due to the Disability Equality Duty for the public sector, which will come into force at the end of 2006 (2005 Disability Discrimination Bill). The general duty applies to all public bodies, including educational establishments, and requires them to actively promote equal opportunities for disabled people. Key bodies, probably including colleges and universities, will have an additional specific duty requiring them to develop, implement and evaluate a disability equality scheme for their organisation, in consultation with disabled people. This represents a shift from the philosophy underlying the 1995 DDA, which is primarily reactive and relies on individual disabled people lodging a complaint of discrimination, towards a more proactive promotion of equality. The public sector duty will also have implications beyond education, of course; perhaps most importantly in its application to employment of disabled people in the public sector.

Further and higher education: widening participation

Part 4 of the DDA also covers further and higher education institutions. Early evidence suggested that these institutions were not well informed about their new duties under the Act and that preparations, such as there had been, had taken the form of policy reviews and disability awareness training rather than substantive changes in practice (DRC, 2003a, 2003b).

Further and higher education institutions may come under pressure from another route, however, since both are being required to widen participation, and disabled people are one of the target groups. The Aimhigher initiative is co-funded by the Higher Education Funding Council for England (HEFCE) and the Department for

Education and Skills, to support outreach work from institutions to school pupils in deprived areas and groups under-represented in higher education. The HEFCE also allocates funding to institutions for capital projects to improve disability access, and to support the development of teaching and learning resources for disabled students. The participation of disabled students in higher education has been monitored since 1994, although at that time the disability status of one third of students was 'unknown'. This proportion has fallen to 2%, making trends difficult to interpret. One can say that the percentage of the total student population *known* to be disabled has risen from 2% in 1994/95 to 5% in 2002/03 (HESA, 2004).

The government has set a target of increasing participation in education at age 17 from 75% to 90% by 2015 (DfES, 2005). This is supported by the Education Maintenance Allowance, a weekly payment of between £10 and £30 per week, paid to 16- to 18-year-olds who are in full-time education after the end of compulsory schooling, if their household income is less than £30,000 per year. Evaluation of the pilot phases of the programme produced encouraging results – it increased participation in the pilot areas by 6 percentage points – and the scheme is now national (Ashworth et al, 2002). Decisions at age 16 are critical to each young person's future trajectory and this report examines them in detail.

Connexions

Connexions was set up between 2001 and 2003 as a new partnership between careers advice services, schools, social services, youth offending teams and other organisations, to provide advice for young people aged 13 to 19. Some evaluations of its effectiveness in joint working have been critical (for example, Coles et al, 2004) and it has not succeeded in reducing the number of 16- to 18-year-olds not in education, training or employment, despite a favourable economic climate. There has been speculation about the future of the service, but at the time of writing a decision has yet to be announced by the government.

One of the difficulties faced by Connexions has been a tension between being a universal service – important to avoid stigmatising young people who use it – but with targets and objectives

focused on the disadvantaged, including disabled people. Models based on using generalist advisers risk allowing young people with complex or less obvious needs to slip through the net, while relying on specialist disability advisers can lead to marginalisation and overuse of a limited range of segregated provision. However, the organisation has begun to address these issues through a series of guidelines on transition planning, working with people with learning difficulties, and partnerships with mental health services (Connexions, 2002, 2003, 2004). Formal advice services are not often cited as influential by young people in the surveys used in this report, but their role is investigated where relevant.

The Social Exclusion Unit has also turned its attention to the support available for 'vulnerable' young people, including those with mental health problems, in the transition from childhood to adulthood (SEU, 2005). Its report identifies three problem areas in service delivery: inflexible age boundaries between services, the need to provide a 'trusted adult' as a guide for a young person across a range of services, and a tendency for service design to ignore the way young people think and behave, for example, by requiring long-term commitment from the start rather than allowing taster sessions or providing more immediate rewards and incentives.

Disabled people's employment

As unemployment has fallen, the government has increasingly turned its attention to groups such as lone parents and disabled people claiming out-of-work benefits, who have traditionally been classified as 'economically inactive' rather than unemployed. The New Deal for Disabled People (NDDP) was piloted in 1998/99, and, despite an ambivalent evaluation, was rolled out nationally (Loumidis et al, 2001). The NDDP has a range of incarnations but key components include a personal adviser with access to a discretionary fund to pay for interview costs, a small amount of training or other interventions that in the adviser's opinion will assist in moving towards work. Participation in the NDDP remains voluntary.

In parallel with the NDDP, a scheme known as 'Pathways to Work' has been piloted, also based on personal advisers, but with the innovation of a Job Preparation Premium of £20 per week conditional on undertaking an agreed programme of activity to assist the return to work, and a return-to-work credit paid at £40 per week for the first year that an ex-claimant is in a job.[5] Early evidence on 'Pathways' is encouraging and the scheme is to be extended to 30 local authority districts and a broader selection of existing Incapacity Benefit (IB) claimants (Johnson, 2005).

The help available via the NDDP and Pathways to Work is additional to financial assistance with costs incurred in employment, through a long-established scheme known as Access to Work (AtW). AtW is mainly tax-funded although co-payments from employers are required in some circumstances. AtW helps with the cost of adaptations to the workplace, special equipment, personal assistance at work (for example a reader for a blind employee), and travel to and from work. Spending on AtW has increased significantly since 1997, although the government is still reluctant to advertise the scheme – perhaps through fear of an explosion of claims – and awareness of its existence among both employers and potential employees remains limited.

At the same time, the delivery of social security to people of working age has been reorganised, so that all claimants, whether disabled, lone parents or unemployed, are now dealt with by Jobcentre Plus. New claimants must attend a work-focused interview as a condition of receipt of benefit (although this requirement can be waived in certain circumstances). For lone parents and disabled people any action arising from the work-focused meeting, such as referral to a New Deal, is voluntary. Delivery of benefits through a single work-focused organisation has the advantage that all claimants are given access to help in looking for work; on the other hand, insertion of an additional stage into the claims process has resulted in a lengthening of the average time between initial contact and first payment of benefit (Karagiannaki, 2005).

Whether as a result of these reforms, or, perhaps more plausibly, as a result of a sustained period of economic growth, disabled people's employment rates overall have risen slightly, from 43% in 1998 to 50% in 2004. Correspondingly, unemployment rates have fallen, and this fall has been much faster for disabled people than for non-disabled people.

The age group most relevant to this report coincides with those eligible for the New Deal for Young People (NDYP), namely 18- to 24-year-olds. The NDYP has reduced youth unemployment, but as Figure 1.2 shows, this has had only a marginal effect on reducing the proportion of this age group not in education, employment or training, and it has not succeeded in narrowing the gap between disabled and non-disabled young people. The rates of disabled men and women in this age group who are unemployed or economically inactive are more than twice as high as those of non-disabled men and women.

Most recently, the government announced its intention to overhaul IB (DWP, 2005). Currently the line between claimants who are required to seek work as a condition of their benefit and those who are not is drawn between Jobseeker's Allowance claimants and IB claimants. The proposal is to shift that line to part way through the IB caseload. Those who are newly classified as being required to seek work will be paid a lower rate of benefit, with premiums paid conditional on their work-related activities. Those who are classified as not being required to seek work will be paid a higher rate of benefit than the current long-term IB rate.

The impact of these reforms will depend crucially on:

(i) how the division between the two groups of claimants is made;
(ii) the nature of the work-seeking requirements and support;
(iii) the rates of the new benefits;
(iv) how easy it will be to move between groups.

All of these details have yet to be determined. The reforms have the potential to break the link between disability and poverty by significantly raising benefit levels for those out of work long term while speeding the return to work of those who wish to do so. However, they also have the

---

[5] The return-to-work credit is paid regardless of the level of earnings. By contrast, the disability component of Working Tax Credit is paid as a supplement to low earnings. Both serve to ensure that a larger proportion of disabled people will have higher incomes in work than out of work.

Figure 1.2: Percentage of 18- to 24-year-olds not in education, employment or training

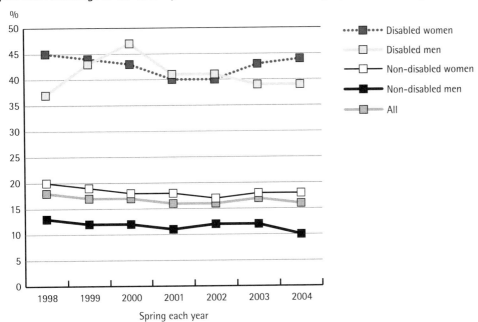

Note: Uses a definition of not in education, employment or training (NEET) based on the respondent's self-reported economic activity and therefore does not correspond to official definitions of NEET.
Source: Author's calculations using quarterly Labour Force Surveys

potential to introduce a new administrative hurdle for disabled claimants to jump, to re-enforce the power of the medical establishment in assessing the capabilities of disabled people, and to condemn some disabled claimants to a choice between accepting a benefit rate well below the poverty line or undergoing a series of humiliating and increasingly pointless job-seeking activities. There is much at stake.

Summary

This Introduction has argued that examining the formation of educational and employment aspirations among disabled and non-disabled young people, and following that through into looking at the prospects for translating those aspirations into reality, is an important part of assessing the degree of autonomy that young disabled people are afforded in our society.

The key questions that will be addressed in the analysis that follows are:

(1) What reasons lie behind the lower educational attainment of disabled young people? To what extent do low aspirations – of the young people themselves or of others – play a part?

(2) What reasons lie behind the poorer labour market experience among disabled people in early adult life? To what extent is this due to their lower educational qualifications, other background characteristics, or to low occupational aspirations?

(3) Has the gap between disabled and non-disabled young people's aspirations narrowed over successive cohorts? What about the gap between their chances of fulfilling their aspirations?

The structure and quality of education is high on the government's agenda, for young people in general, and specifically for those with SEN. In employment, high rates of economic inactivity among disabled people, including young disabled people, have become a target for government intervention. At the same time, disabled people's rights are being increasingly recognised legislatively in education and employment. It would be overly optimistic to think that policies have yet created an environment of equality of opportunity for disabled and non-disabled young people, but whether the gap between the two groups has begun to close is the subject for this research.

2

Aspirations

Young people's aspirations are a critical ingredient in achievement in education and in occupational outcomes later in life. Skills, qualifications and experience are important factors too, but without self-belief and encouragement, they are all too likely not to be attained in the first place, or not to be put to good use.

Research on how those in their mid-teens think about the future has consistently found that further education, employment, leaving home and starting a family are the chief preoccupations (Morrow and Richards, 1996). While all these areas of life are important, this report focuses mainly on education and employment. As Bynner (1998, p 29) has argued, "Of all the developmental transitions, entry to employment is probably the most central to the formation of adult identity".

This chapter begins by looking at what is known about the influences on the formation of aspirations among young people in general, and among disabled people in particular. The various possible influences are drawn together in a framework that is used later to guide the analysis. The aspirations expressed by disabled and non-disabled young people are then described, drawing on two data sources: 16-year-olds from the 1970 British Cohort Study (BCS70), and 16/17-year-olds from cohorts 9 and 10 of the Youth Cohort Studies (YCS). The data sources were described in Chapter 1 and more details are available in the Appendix.

What influences the formation of aspirations?

Psychologists tend to emphasise the importance of character traits and personal identity in the formation of aspirations (Haller and Miller, 1971).

According to this school of thought, occupational choice and career development is essentially a process of developing and implementing a 'self-concept' (Watts et al, 1981). Young people who are least fatalistic in their outlook are most likely to be successful in staying on in education or gaining employment (Banks et al, 1992).

Sociologists have drawn attention to the role of characteristics such as gender, ethnicity and social class. Although there has been some convergence between boys and girls since the 1970s in the jobs they identify as desirable, strong gender differences remain (Kelly, 1989; Schoon, 2001; Schoon and Parsons, 2002). Differences between minority ethnic groups are complex, with children from Asian, especially Indian, backgrounds showing greater tendency to want to continue in education and achieve higher-status occupations (Raby and Walford, 1981), but children from Caribbean ethnic backgrounds tending to be more disaffected.

Often the same factor influences the formation of aspirations and the chances the young person has of achieving their goals: for example, being from a higher social class background is associated with higher occupational aspirations, and is also associated with a higher likelihood of achieving the occupation of choice (Furlong, 1992).

Peer group, parental and teacher expectations are important influences on a young person (Schoon, 2001; Schoon and Parsons, 2002). The evidence on the impact of the school environment has been more mixed, however, with some studies finding little school-specific effect (Raby and Walford, 1981).

Prior educational achievement is important at every stage. A young person who already has some academic success will be more motivated to acquire further qualifications and skills, and will also be in a better position to access those opportunities (Furlong, 1992; Schoon and Parsons, 2002). Conversely, lack of success or recognition at school can produce a downwards spiral.

An economic perspective emphasises the importance of local labour market conditions, both in terms of the motivation they may give to young people and in terms of the actual opportunities available to them (Carter, 1962; Raby and Walford, 1981; Bynner, 1998). Cross-national evidence suggests that higher rates of youth unemployment are associated with a slight *increase* in staying-on rates at 16, principally because other opportunities are limited (McIntosh, 2001). However, the effect is small in relation to the effect of the individual's prior academic attainment.

Aspirations develop through the teenage years: 'fantasy' occupations such as pop star and astronaut become less common, and early experience of the labour market puts a further dampener on some young people's ambitions (Kelly, 1989; Furlong, 1992).

Disabled young people's aspirations

A small number of studies have looked at disabled young people's aspirations in the context of the transition from school to adulthood. Morris (1999a) found that young people with complex health and support needs had very similar aspirations to young people in general – they wanted to be able to choose to live independently when they felt ready, to socialise with their friends, and to do something useful. But in practice many were at risk of moving into institutional accommodation, losing contact with friends and had low educational achievements, which would put them at a significant disadvantage in the labour market.

The National Child Development Study follows all children born in a particular week in 1958. Walker (1982) used this study to compare the experiences of disabled and non-disabled young people. The proportion of disabled youngsters who aspired to semi-skilled and unskilled jobs was six times the proportion of non-disabled young people with those aspirations. Despite these modest aspirations, only one fifth of disabled 18-year-olds had achieved the

occupational group of the job they had desired at age 16, compared to one third of non-disabled youngsters. Walker also found that the gap between aspirations and outcomes widened as the 'careers' of the young people progressed. A spell of unemployment had the effect of further reducing aspirations.

A study of teenagers with cerebral palsy or spina bifida made interesting comparisons between those attending mainstream school and those at special school (Anderson and Clarke, 1982). The disabled youngsters in mainstream education were just as likely as their non-disabled counterparts to want to get a job when they left education (around two fifths of each group), whereas those attending special school were more likely to respond with 'don't know' or to say that they wanted to attend a day centre. By the age of 19, however, only 17% of those who had attended mainstream school and had cerebral palsy or spina bifida had secured employment, and even fewer among those who had attended special school. A follow-up study when these young people were age 25 (Clark and Hirst, 1989) found only half of all those who had wanted to get a job were working, and most were still hoping to achieve what they regarded as full adult status.

The Department for Education and Skills (DfES) is currently funding a longitudinal study of young people with special educational needs (SEN). So far, they have been interviewed in Year 11 (approximately age 16) and two years later (Polat et al, 2001; Dewson et al, 2004). The sample includes those with and without statements, in mainstream or special school, and with a range of impairments, including cognitive impairments. The study has revealed divergent experiences of transition. Young people with sensory and/or physical impairments were generally well-catered for in terms of multi-agency involvement in planning and providing a pathway to continue education. There were, however, questions for this group about whether the routes they are pursuing allow for genuine progression, or just 'treading water'. By contrast, the larger group of young people with mild learning difficulties, or with behavioural or emotional problems, were less likely to have significant support in making a transition after 16, and were more likely to have drifted out of education and to be unemployed or in low-paid work.

Disabled identity and resilience

Despite these difficulties, many disabled young people are resilient and formulate positive aspirations. Research in schools has identified a number of different mechanisms disabled children use to resist the stereotypes and roles into which they are placed, and to deal with the reactions of fellow pupils and teachers to their impairment (Lightfoot et al, 1999; Priestley, 1999). Students sometimes adopt a 'disabled identity' to ensure that their needs are recognised and met, but that does not mean giving up their identity as children or young adults (Low, 1996). Enjoying a degree of autonomy and gaining experience at making decisions are important mechanisms for boosting self-esteem and engendering a belief in one's ability to shape one's future (Hirst and Baldwin, 1994; Cowen, 2001).

Some of the disabled people interviewed for this study reported having developed their own strategies for getting by at school.[6] For example, one young man with a visual impairment had gained respect from his fellow pupils by helping the less academically able with their class work. He described academic work as a 'refuge' from bullying.

Parents

Relations between parents and their offspring during the transition from childhood to adulthood can be fraught in the best of circumstances. Disabled young people and their parents may find themselves in a particularly difficult situation. For example, Skelton and Valentine (2002) found that the parents of Deaf young people were a key source of support but also could also be overprotective. The extended period of transition some young people in the study needed placed additional strain on relationships. In another study, parents of children attending special school expressed a desire to encourage the aspirations or their son or daughter but they also feared disappointment if aspirations rose above likely outcomes (Mitchell, 1999). This coincided with professionals' judgements, which tended to be based on what was "regarded as feasible or just 'being realistic'" (p 757).

---

6   See Chapter 1 for interview methodology.

Children with less well-educated parents may face additional barriers to educational achievement. In some cases parents try to give encouragement, but themselves lack the knowledge or education to make an effective intervention (Preece, 1996). Where it is necessary to negotiate with education and health authorities, and possibly with social services, to ensure that the best equipment and support is in place for the child, parents who are less confident in dealing with professionals may be at a disadvantage (Morris, 2002). 'Exceptional parents' – exceptional in the material, social and emotional resources they provide – can be the key to a successful transition to employment and independent living (Pascall and Hendey, 2004).

Young people interviewed for the DfES study of transitions among people with SEN were most likely to say that their parents had been the most helpful in making decisions about what to do post-16 (Dewson et al, 2004). Similarly, the young disabled people interviewed for this study had relied on parents and other family members for advice, practical support and lobbying power during their time at school and beyond. Most felt their parents had been encouraging, although several mentioned that when the time came to leave home or to travel further afield, parents had more concerns about the practicalities. One young Deaf woman had found an ally in her social worker, who intervened to persuade the parents that she was capable of a greater degree of independence.

School and beyond

The impact of the school environment and of teachers on disabled young people can be positive or negative. In a review of disability discrimination in education, Gray (2002) reported that stereotyping of some disabled children by teachers remained a problem, as did under-expectation of their academic abilities. Difficulties at an institutional level included admission policies, physical access, segregation for part or all of the time, and delays in appropriate support being provided. This was confirmed by a survey of disabled 16- to 24-year-olds (Wilson, 2003). More than one in five reported that they had been discouraged from taking particular options at school, one in five had been discouraged from taking GCSEs, one in eight had been discouraged from taking A/AS levels, and a similar proportion had been discouraged from taking vocational qualifications. One quarter said that they had been advised not to go on to further or higher education by their schools. On the other hand, nearly three quarters felt that their teachers had valued their achievements and progress in the same way as for other pupils.

Positive and negative experiences at school were reported by the disabled people interviewed for this study.

Positive:

- good teachers;
- being encouraged academically;
- a safe environment;
- learning support assistants provided by the local education authority.

Negative:

- bullying/social isolation;
- discouragement/being undermined by peer group;
- staff who felt they knew best;
- being singled out for special treatment;
- poor-quality teaching;
- teachers underestimating academic potential;
- special school 'too cosy';
- arguments with the local education authority about which secondary school could be made accessible.

The transition from school to further or higher education had been universally difficult among those interviewed for this study who had made such a move. The problems mentioned included:

- being 'left to get on with it' at sixth-form college, with insufficient support;
- a big jump between school and further education college;
- felt like 'starting from square one';
- fears about fitting in at the new institution;
- feeling sick with nerves on starting university.

The choice of further or higher education institution was sometimes limited by the additional difficulties of living away from the parental home:

- parental concerns about safety, travel and practical coping if moved away from home;

- leaving home (and dealing with social services) too much to cope with at the same time as starting university: "I couldn't stand them mucking up my chance of getting out in the world by getting a degree";
- reduced choice of university if have to continue living at home.

Sources of advice

Although legislation is in place to ensure that young people with a statement of SEN have advice and support in the process of leaving compulsory education, a recent study found that less than half of its sample of 18/19-year-olds with SEN could remember having had a transition planning meeting (Dewson et al, 2004). These young people felt that their parents had been the most helpful source of advice and support, followed by staff at school, with careers advisers and Connexions coming in last.

Lack of support or perceived lack of support is a problem for both mainstream and special school pupils. Teenagers coming up to school-leaving age in a study based in special schools expressed clear ideas about the occupations to which they aspired, but made few specific references to ways and means of moving towards these goals (Norwich, 1997).

Sources of advice other than family members mentioned by the young people interviewed for this study included:

- family friend;
- social worker;
- British Sign Language (BSL) communicator;
- A level teachers;
- staff at a Community Arts Project.

Interactions with other forms of disadvantage

Disability interacts with other forms of disadvantage (Lakey et al, 2001; Berthoud, 2003). The Black and disabled young people interviewed by Bignall and Butt (2000) had similar aspirations to their non-disabled counterparts but had in some cases experienced double discrimination in pursuing their goals, on account of their ethnicity and their disability. Among the British South Asian families studied by Hussain (2003), disabled young people were given less scope for combining Western with traditional culture than their non-disabled

Box 2.1: Factors that influence the formation of educational and occupational aspirations

Personal
- age
- gender
- ethnicity
- impairment (severity, type, age at onset)
- health
- self-esteem
- self-perception of disability
- 'locus of control'

Parental
- aspirations/expectations
- interest in school/homework
- own education
- own occupation/social class
- supportiveness

Peer group
- aspirations of peer group
- bullying

Personal history
- previous educational achievement
- work experience

School characteristics
- type of school
- attitudes of teachers
- careers advice
- availability of specialist support

Local conditions
- unemployment rate
- existence of further and higher education colleges

Note: any of these factors may interact.

siblings, and less importance was placed on their education. Preece (1996) argues that social class was a key determinant of the expected outcomes for disabled young people in mainstream and special schools: children from working-class backgrounds were not encouraged to strive for academic achievement at school, the objective was purely vocational.

Box 2.1 pulls together the evidence on the influences on the formation of educational and occupational aspirations, drawing on the existing literature and the interviews carried out for this study. Indicators for the majority of these factors are available directly or indirectly in the two datasets used for analysis, and the framework represented in Figure 1.1 in the Introduction will be used in the following chapter to examine the influences on aspirations. First, however, the aspirations of disabled and non-disabled young people are described and compared.

Aspirations among the 1970 birth cohort at age 16

As described in Chapter 1, the BCS70 collects information from parents and from health professionals about the disability status of the 16-year-old cohort members. Where the information given is inconsistent, the young person is

categorised in the tables and figures below as having 'uncertain status'. In all likelihood, these young people have less severe impairments than those who are reported as disabled by both parents and health professionals, but it could also be that they have impairments whose effect is noticeable in one context but not in another.

Table 2.1 reports the intentions of the 16-year-olds with respect to staying on in education. Three questions are asked at different points in the survey that have a bearing on this, and although the majority of responses are consistent there are some that are not. Around three fifths of each of the three groups (non-disabled, disabled and uncertain status) consistently say they want to remain in education.[7]

Looking in more detail at those who want to stay on, a higher proportion of disabled young people are staying on in order to (re-)take O levels and CSEs (19%), than are non-disabled (12%), and correspondingly fewer are staying on to take A levels.[8]

---

[7] Pupils at special schools often expect to stay on beyond the age of 16 and this does not necessarily signify higher-level courses. Unfortunately there are too few pupils at special school in the sample to analyse this separately.

[8] The year is 1986; GCSEs were introduced in 1988.

When asked why they are intending to leave full-time education, the reasons given by non-disabled young people are more strongly weighted towards the positive (for example, 'I want to earn to gain independence', 'I want to go elsewhere to complete my training') than the reasons given by disabled young people (for example, 'I have always taken it for granted', 'My teacher advised me to leave').[9]

Young people are also asked what they would like to do after this school year, as opposed to what they expect to do (Table 2.2). They are offered a list of options, including getting a job or undertaking training. Again, the aspirations of disabled and non-disabled young people are broadly similar, although in this context, fewer disabled young people say they want to continue

in full-time education and a higher proportion say they want to do vocational training (not statistically significant). Slightly more disabled young people say they 'don't know' what they want to do next, compared to non-disabled young people.

The survey also asks where the young person sees themselves in five years' time (that is, at age 21). Table 2.3 presents the results. Disabled young people are more likely than their non-disabled counterparts to think that they will be studying in five years' time (a view that is not entirely consistent with the smaller proportion of disabled young people who are expecting to stay on to take A levels, although they may be expecting to be continuing with secondary-level qualifications), but less likely to see themselves

Table 2.1: Intention to leave education at age 16 (%)

Will leave education this year	Non-disabled	Uncertain status	Disabled
No – stay on	59.8	61.5	61.9
Yes – leave	33.3	31.6	31.0
Don't know/gives contradictory answers	6.8	6.9	7.1
Total	100.0	100.0	100.0
Number of respondents	*4,952*	*247*	*84*

Note: Differences between 'non-disabled' and (i) uncertain status, or (ii) disabled, are not statistically significant.[10]
Source: BCS70 age 16 survey

Table 2.2: Immediate plans (%)

What do you want to do after this school year?	Non-disabled	Uncertain status	Disabled
Full-time education	45.6	49.1	37.1
Vocational training	10.0	12.3	14.3
Job	26.8	22.2	28.6
YTS/unemployment	14.0	13.2	12.9
Don't know	3.6	3.3	7.1
Total	100.0	100.0	100.0
Number of respondents	*3,980*	*212*	*70*

Notes: 'YTS' is Youth Training Scheme, a government-funded training programme for young people who would otherwise be unemployed.
Differences in the proportion who want to remain in full-time education between 'non-disabled' and (i) uncertain status, or (ii) disabled, are not statistically significant.
Source: BCS70 age 16 survey

---

9   Based on a list of 12 possible reasons, with multiple responses allowed. Positive = earn independence, can't study subject I want to at school, have a particular course in mind, want to leave home, want to get married, want to complete training elsewhere. Negative = always taken it for granted, need to earn, most of my friends are leaving, parental advice, teachers' advice, I'm not bright enough.

10   Unless otherwise specified, statistical significance is given at the 95% level, assessed using a t-test. 'Statistically significant at 95%', means that if the survey were repeated for the same population, no difference between the two groups compared in the relevant respect would be found in five out of 100 times.

Table 2.3: Longer-term plans (%)

In five years' time what will you be doing?	Non-disabled	Uncertain status	Disabled
Studying at university or polytechnic	17.6	17.4	25.0
Working ...			
in a profession	35.0	35.3	23.8
in an office	16.7	13.3	16.3
in a skilled trade	10.4	10.6	8.8
with my hands	8.3	10.1	10.0
in the open air	3.4	2.3	5.0
Something else	8.6	11.0	11.3
Total	100.0	100.0	100.0
Number of respondents	*4,495*	*218*	*80*

Source: BCS70 age 16 survey

in a profession. The proportions of disabled and non-disabled young people in these two categories together are similar. Other categories are also similar across disability status sub-groups, although a slightly higher proportion of disabled young people think they will be doing 'something else', presumably unemployed or looking after the home or family.

One of the most interesting questions in the age 16 survey asks the young people 'What do you want to do in life?' and gives a list of 15 occupations. Those who tick 'Job not included above' are invited to give more details, and these provide a fascinating – and sometimes amusing – insight into the respondents' aspirations. One young disabled woman replied that she was going to be a "megastar female vocalist", while among the non-disabled there were a budding astronaut, a very large number of would-be air hostesses, and several aspiring footballers. At the more modest end of the spectrum, one non-disabled young person responded, "any job, you can't pick and choose these days", while a disabled young person said, "will depend on my disability". Some young people did not envisage themselves having a paid job at all: they expected to be unemployed, being a housewife,

Table 2.4: Summary of occupational aspirations (%)

What do you want to do in life?	Non-disabled	Uncertain status	Disabled
Professional; senior government	24.3	26.8	32.9
Professional and related in education, welfare and health	13.5	11.2	9.6
Literary, artistic and sports	1.9	2.7	0.0
Clerical and related	21.1	16.1	19.2
Selling	4.6	4.5	5.5
Security and protective services	6.6	5.4	4.1
Catering, cleaning, hairdressing and other personal services	9.9	12.1	9.6
Farming, fishing and related	3.2	4.5	5.5
Materials processing; making and repairing (excluding metal and electrical)	6.6	7.6	6.9
Processing, making, repairing and related (metal and electrical)	4.8	4.0	2.7
Painting, repetitive assembling, product inspecting, packaging and related	1.0	1.3	2.7
Construction, mining and related	0.7	1.3	0.0
Transport operating, materials moving and storing and related	1.4	2.7	1.4
Other	0.6	0.0	0.0
Total	100.0	100.0	100.0
Number of respondents	*4,544*	*224*	*73*

Note: The correspondence between the occupations listed in the questionnaire and the CO80 listed here is approximate. CO80 class 4 (professionals in science, etc) is here included under class 1; CO80 class 5 (managerial) is here included under class 2.
Source: BCS70 age 16 survey

or, in one case, "none, because I already have a baby".

A summary table (see Table 2.4) cannot do justice to the imagination and thought that the young people had in many cases given to their future occupations, but for the purposes of this study, the jobs described have been coded, as best as possible, to fit the standard Classification of Occupations used at the time (1980) (CO80).[11] The fit is imperfect because the categories given in the survey questionnaire do not match CO80 categories exactly and because the young people's free text responses vary in the amount of detail given, but it does give a broad idea of the kinds of occupations for which young people were looking.

Table 2.4 shows that many disabled young people are aiming high: nearly one third aspire to a professional occupation or to senior positions in government. This is a higher proportion than among non-disabled young people. Slightly more non-disabled young people than disabled want to work in education, welfare or health (including the popular categories of teaching and nursing). Overall, the distribution within each

disability status is similar and, cumulatively, the difference in occupational aspirations of disabled and non-disabled young people is not statistically significant.

Figure 2.1 summarises this information yet further, by relating occupations to social class. Again, the match is approximate because in many cases we do not have information about whether the young person is thinking of becoming a manager or just a worker in a particular sector. The figure confirms that disabled young people are more likely than their non-disabled counterparts to be aiming for professional social-class jobs, although they are less likely to be aiming for managerial and technical occupations. Overall, the distribution is similar and there is not a statistically significant difference between them.

Respondents are asked to rate their prospects, relative to their contemporaries, of getting a job when the time comes, on a scale from 1 (much less likely) to 5 (much more likely). Specifically, they are asked whether they think their health or educational qualifications will be an obstacle to getting their desired job (1 = yes, 2= no). They are also asked to consider what strengths they

Figure 2.1: Occupational aspirations at age 16 (%)

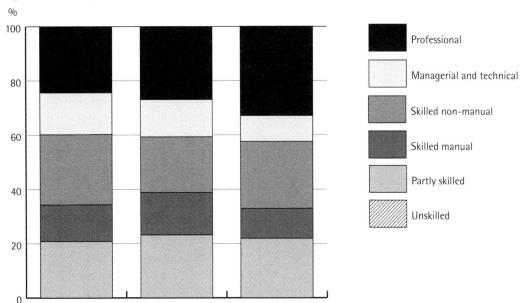

Note: The correspondence between social class and occupational categories is approximate. No respondents are coded as aspiring to 'unskilled' occupations because all of the categories listed in the survey questionnaire include at least some partly skilled occupations.
Source: BCS70 age 16 survey

---

[11] My thanks to Laura Lane for help with coding the occupation questions.

Table 2.5: Self-assessed job prospects and personal attributes[a]

Average score	Non-disabled	Uncertain status	Disabled
Relative job prospects (1 = much less likely than contemporaries, to 5 = much more likely)	3.42	3.33	3.25[*]
Health/education no obstacle (1=yes, 2=no)	1.91	1.81	1.55[**]
Locus of control (index ranges 33 to 78)	60.3	59.7	57.8[*]
Self-esteem (index ranges 0 to 20)	15.1	14.5[*]	14.3[*]

Notes:

[a] Each indicator is constructed so that a higher value reflects a more positive attitude.

Difference between non-disabled and this category is statistically significant at *90% level, **95% level.

Source: BCS70 age 16 survey

have in seeking a job, from a list of eight possible characteristics (for example, reliability, responsibility, tidiness). A further block of questions ask about attitudes towards fate and individual agency, responses to which can be used to construct a locus of control scale (Rotter, 1966). A high score indicates someone who has an internal locus of control – they feel that their actions make a difference and that effort will be rewarded; the opposite end of the scale represents a more fatalistic outlook. Finally, another set of questions has been designed to measure self-esteem. Table 2.5 gives the mean values for each by disability status.[12]

Although the absolute differences are not large, the results tell a consistent story. Disabled young people are aware that their health or education may be a barrier to getting the job they want, and they rate their job prospects less favourably than their peers. They feel less confident of their ability to control their fate and have slightly lower self-esteem. Of course there is considerable variation within each disability status group as well, but the fact that the difference between the mean scores on each indicator reaches statistical significance, suggests that there is a general tendency for disabled young people to feel less confident.

The analysis of young people's aspirations thus far shows disabled 16-year-olds keen to stay on in education and aiming high in the labour market, in a similar way to their non-disabled counterparts. Their expectations are more

hesitant, however: they are not confident that they will be able to bring their ambitions to fruition.

Aspirations of young people born in the early 1980s

The YCS offer a more up-to-date, although less detailed, picture of the outlook of 16- and 17-year-olds than that provided by BCS70. Here we use cohorts 9 and 10 for which sweep 1 (age 16/17) took place in spring 1998 and spring 2000 respectively.[13]

As discussed in Chapter 1, the YCS contain broad information about disability status but do not allow us to distinguish either type or severity of impairment. With this limitation in mind, the results in Figure 2.2 compare the attitudes and aspirations of disabled and non-disabled young people. Just under one in 20 (4.8%) of the combined sample for the two cohorts report that they are disabled.

YCS respondents are asked questions at various points in the survey about how well they feel school has equipped them for the future, and how they feel about their prospects in general. The statements to which they are invited to 'agree' or 'disagree' are:

(1) School has helped give me confidence to make decisions.
(2) School has done little to prepare me for life when I leave school.

---

[12] These questions occur at different points in the questionnaire, not consecutively, and in the original are coded so that a positive attitude corresponds to a high value on some questions and a low value on others.

[13] The sampling frame for YCS is based on schools so it does not include those educated at home.

Figure 2.2: Distribution of 16/17-year-olds by pay expected from full-time job

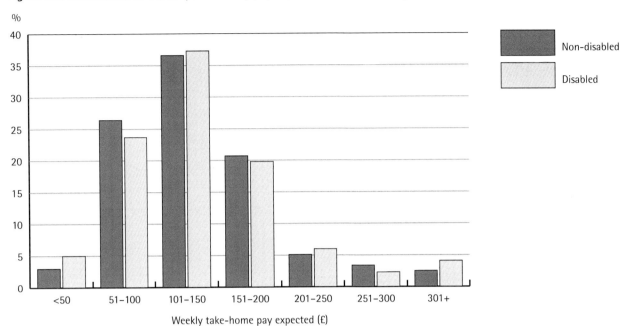

Note: Results weighted using weights supplied with the data.
Source: YCS cohort 9 sweep 1 and cohort 10 sweep 1

(3) School has taught me things which would be useful in a job.
(4) School work was generally worth doing.
(5) I think that making plans for the future is a waste of time.
(6) I get enough support in planning my future.
(7) I know how to find out about future work, training or education opportunities.

By recoding so that a positive attitude with respect to any statement scores 1 and a negative attitude scores 0, and then summing for all seven statements, an index can be created indicating the confidence with which the young person is facing the future. On such an index, non-disabled young people score an average of 5.5 compared to 5.2 for disabled young people, and this difference is highly statistically significant. Non-disabled young people are more positive with respect to each individual item of the index and the magnitudes of the differences between them and disabled youngsters are similar across items.

Respondents who are not currently in full-time work are invited to say, (a) what weekly take-home pay they would expect to get from a full-time job, and (b) the minimum weekly take-

home pay they would be willing to accept.[14] Here disabled respondents appear to be more optimistic: they give an average figure of £162 in response to the first question, compared to an average of £152 for non-disabled (difference not statistically significant). Closer examination reveals that the median figure given by each group is the same (£140) and that disabled people are both more likely to give very low figures (less than £50 per week) and to give very high figures (more than £300 per week) (Figure 2.2). This could reflect a comparative lack of knowledge about the world of work.

In terms of the 'reservation wage', as it is sometimes called, again the difference between the average figure given by disabled and non-disabled young people is not statistically significant. The distribution shows a similar pattern to Figure 2.2: 22% of disabled respondents would accept a job paying less than

---

14 Cohort 9 are invited to fill in their own figure. Cohort 10 are invited to indicate into which of 10 bands of weekly take-home pay their figure falls into. Averages reported here therefore refer to cohort 9 only, while the distribution shown in Figure 2.2 uses data from both cohorts.

£50 per week (compared to 17% of non-disabled young people), but 2% set their minimum threshold as high as £301 per week (compared to 1% of non-disabled young people).

It is interesting to note that if a full-time job is taken to be 35 hours per week, the minimum wage rate for 18- to 21-year-olds at the time of the cohort 10 sweep 1 survey (early 2000) would have fallen into the £101-£150 bracket.[15] Among both disabled and non-disabled young people, nearly one in three (29%) would have accepted a job below this level.

Summary

The first part of this chapter canvassed the importance of aspirations in shaping a young person's future, and also the influences on the formation of aspirations. The second and third parts of the chapter offered a picture of disabled young people's aspirations and compared them to their non-disabled counterparts. It showed disabled young people generally aiming high: wanting to stay on in education, gain qualifications, get high-status jobs and earn a good wage. These were very similar aspirations to non-disabled people of the same age.

On the other hand, disabled people at age 16 were generally less confident and felt less well-equipped to tackle the transition into adulthood, as indicated by a number of subjective measures. This finding emerged from both the earlier survey (BCS70 in 1986), and the later surveys (YCS in 1998/2000).

This conclusion differs from that reached by Walker's research based on an earlier survey of young people who turned 16 in 1974 (Walker, 1982). Among that cohort, the occupational aspirations of physically disabled young people were significantly lower than those of the non-disabled group. This contrast gives rise to the idea that changes in society over the intervening period, and perhaps more specifically, changes in education – a move towards greater integration of disabled children into mainstream schools and the advent of comprehensive education – could be responsible for narrowing the gap in the aspirations of disabled and non-disabled young people.

Before we can give greater credence to that idea, however, it is important to examine other possible influences on aspirations and how these differ between disabled and non-disabled teenagers – a task to which the next chapter turns.

---

[15] The minimum wage was introduced in April 1999, ie after the cohort 9 sweep 1 survey. Note also that the minimum wage does not apply to 16- and 17-year-olds.

3

Aiming high?

The previous chapter outlined the aspirations 16-year-olds expressed for their future education and employment. It showed that disabled young people had broadly similar objectives to their non-disabled peers, sometimes aiming even higher. However, their confidence about being able to achieve those aspirations was lower, on the whole, and their expectations were correspondingly reduced.

This chapter explores the variation in aspirations by other characteristics as well as disability, such as gender, ethnicity and social class. It seeks to examine whether the differences (and similarities) between disabled and non-disabled young people hold after controlling for other characteristics. It also investigates whether or not these other characteristics make more of a difference to the aspirations of disabled young people than to non-disabled young people.

Contrasting stories

Before turning to the statistical analysis, it may be helpful to keep in mind that each individual has their own story to tell. Boxes 3.1 and 3.2 describe the aspirations of two disabled young people with contrasting circumstances. They are real cases drawn from the 1970 British Cohort Study (BCS70) sample, and all the information is as reported by the young person, their parents or the professionals who completed survey questionnaires about them.[16] Their names, of course, are fictional.

Variation in aspirations by key characteristics

This section explores the extent to which different characteristics are associated with higher or lower aspirations. The first sets of results look at one characteristic at a time; at the end of the section a multivariate regression controls for several different characteristics simultaneously.

Nature of impairment

This section is relevant only for young people who are disabled. The number of individuals in each subset about whom the relevant information is available (for example, young people with severe impairments who want to stay on in education) is often small, so these results must be treated as indicative rather than conclusive. Due to the small numbers, few of the differences are statistically significant.

- Staying on in education
  Those with more severe impairments seem to be more likely to say that they intend to stay on in education after the age of 16. Among those who intend to stay on, those with more severe impairments are more likely to want to do vocational courses. Young people with mental health problems are less likely than other disabled young people to want to stay on.

- Expectations for five years' time
  If expectations for five years' time are ordered from expecting to be at university or polytechnic, through the occupations from professional to working in the open air, with 'doing something else' as a final category (see Table 2.3 in Chapter 2, p 16), young people's expectations can be judged as higher or lower. Obviously this is not intended to imply a value judgement about any individual's aspiration.

---

[16] My thanks to Abigail McKnight for illustrating to me the potential for this approach.

Box 3.1: Dan, at age 16

Dan is White, an only child, who lives with his mother in an owner-occupied house. She left school at 16 but is now studying part time. Dan's father, who was educated to degree level, died when Dan was 10. Dan has a sight impairment, which the nurse considers results in 'some interference' with his daily life, and some facial disfigurement.

He attends mainstream school and has a generally positive attitude to school and school work, although friendships are more problematic: he often feels lonely, and thinks other children often say nasty things about him. He says he has often felt anxious or depressed in the last year. He has never had a girlfriend (or boyfriend), but he does have a best friend at school.

Dan's mother reports that he has had eating problems in the past and that he is rather solitary in his habits. Dan's mother herself sometimes feels low and worried, but overall she has a high self-esteem.

Dan wants to stay on at school and go on to higher education. He has received some careers advice from school (but no work experience) and is aiming for a professional career. His ideal job would be a bank manager. He has both family and other contacts who he thinks could help him get the job of his choice. All in all he thinks it will be fairly easy to get a job, although he recognises that his 'health' may be a barrier.

Dan is highly motivated and a firm believer in his ability to control his own fate (his 'locus of control' score is above the 98th percentile for all young people in the BCS70 sample). He believes he has a number of strengths that will help him in the labour market. In five years' time, he thinks he will be working in an office.

His mother also hopes and expects him to stay on in education. She is pleased with his progress at school and how he is turning out. She is not especially involved in his education, however: she has been to his school just once since last year and Dan does not feel she gives him much help with his homework. His rating of her overall supportiveness is low in comparison to other young people (in the bottom twentieth), and he is more likely to confide in a friend about a range of personal problems than in his mother. He is thinking of leaving home 'now or very soon'.

The family is on a very low income – under £50 per week according to Dan's mother. Dan receives £3 per week pocket money from his mother (the median value for all children) and does not have a job. He feels he does not have enough money but recognises that his mother would give more if she could. He often misses out on things like fashionable clothes, going to the cinema and going out with friends. He is saving up for a bike or a moped.

Box 3.2: Janine, at age 16

Janine is White and is the youngest of three children. She lives with both her parents in a house they are buying with a mortgage. Her father left school at the earliest opportunity and with no qualifications, but her mother got some O levels. Janine's father has a skilled manual job in the textile industry and her mother has an irregular manual job in a school. Janine has spina bifida (a condition that you are born with), which produces a number of impairments: musculo-skeletal, cardio-vascular and gastro-intestinal, adding up to what the nurse described as a 'marked' disability. She has been assessed as having special educational needs (SEN) and attends a special school.

Janine is very keen on school (in the top tenth of the distribution of attitudinal scores). She has a low self-esteem (in the bottom quarter of the distribution) but does not often feel depressed or anxious. She has several good friends at school and although she does not have a steady boyfriend (or girlfriend) at the moment, she has done in the past.

By contrast, Janine's mother reports that Janine is rather solitary, often worried, frequently bites her finger nails and is sometimes fussy. She says Janine often finds it difficult to concentrate. Janine's mother herself is in indifferent mental health, with frequent sleep problems and anxiety.

Janine wants to stay on in education next year to do some vocational training, although she is not yet sure where. She would like to stay on beyond 18 and perhaps train to become a teacher; certainly in the long run she would like a professional job. However, she thinks it will be fairly difficult to get a job when the time comes and her expectation is that in five years' time, she will have a job that mainly involves working with her hands.

She is modest about the strengths she brings to the labour market (reporting the median number of strengths for the sample). She has experienced unfair treatment in the past, and thinks that her health or education may present difficulties for her achieving her future objectives. She is slightly less sure than the average respondent of her ability to make things happen if she wants to.

The school provided some information to Janine on future training and careers, and she has had some contact with a careers teacher. She was not offered any work experience through the school and has never had a paid job.

Janine's parents are not satisfied with her progress at school although they are fairly pleased with the school itself, the interest the teachers take in Janine, and the advice and communication they have had from the school. The mother hopes Janine will go on to do a vocational course but does not know what to expect. Janine's teacher also thinks she would benefit from staying on in education.

The family income is between £150 and £199 per week, and they are reasonably comfortable financially. Janine does not get any regular pocket money from her parents but she does not feel she misses out on anything as a result.

Those who report a greater number of conditions have lower expectations for where they will be in five years' time, as do those with mental health problems. Young people who became disabled at a younger age (less than five years old) have more positive expectations than those who became disabled later in life (ages 11-16).

- Occupational aspiration
  Using the classification of occupational aspirations based on social class, young people with mental health problems have lower occupational aspirations than other disabled young people. Young people who became disabled after the age of five have lower occupational aspirations than those who became disabled earlier.

A fairly consistent pattern with respect to the nature of impairment emerges across different measures of aspiration: young people with mental health problems, those with more severe impairments or more complex needs, and those who became disabled later in childhood, are all likely to have lower aspirations than other disabled young people.

Gender and ethnicity

This section includes both disabled and non-disabled young people. All differences reported here are statistically significant. Disability status and gender or ethnicity may act to compound (or mitigate) disadvantage; interactions are considered in the discussion following Table 3.1.

- Girls are more likely than boys to want to stay on in education.
- Young people from an Indian, Pakistani or Bangladeshi, or 'Other' ethnic background are more likely than White young people to want to stay on in education. The aspirations of young Black people are not significantly different from their White counterparts in this respect.[17]

- Although girls are more likely to think that they will be 'doing something else' in five years' time, they are on average more positive in their medium-term expectations. They are more likely than boys to see themselves in a profession or working in an office; boys are more likely to expect to be working in a skilled trade in five years' time or at a university/polytechnic.
- Very few Black young people expect to be at a university or polytechnic in five years' time, but on the other hand a higher proportion than any other ethnic group expect to be working in a profession. Their average expectation is not significantly different from their White counterparts.

- Young people from an Indian or 'other' ethnic background have higher medium-term expectations on average than White young people.

- Girls have higher occupational aspirations (classified by social class) than boys.
- Young people from Indian, Pakistani or Bangladeshi, or 'Other' ethnic backgrounds have higher occupational aspirations than their White peers. Black young people have similar aspirations to their White counterparts.

Parental social class and education

Parental social class and parental education are very strong influences on young people's aspirations, for disabled and non-disabled alike. Figure 3.1 shows the strong gradient in educational aspirations of young people with respect to their parents' educational background. Young people who have parents neither of whom have any educational qualifications are more than four times as likely to intend to leave education at 16 than young people who have at least one parent educated to degree level. Conversely, the latter group are five times as likely to expect to be attending a university or polytechnic in five years' time as the former. This strong association between parents' education and the young person's aspirations is similar for disabled and non-disabled young people.

A similar gradient can be observed with respect to parental social class. Teenagers whose parents are in social class I or II are nearly twice as likely to say they are intending to stay on in education as their counterparts whose parents are from social class IV or V.

These differences carry through into occupational aspirations. Half of all young people with parents educated to degree level aspire to a professional occupation, as do 44% of young people with parents in social class I or II. These figures compare to just 14% of young people with parents who have no educational qualifications and 16% of young people with parents in social class IV or V, respectively.

---

[17] The pre-coded categories for ethnicity in BCS70 at age 16 were: English/Welsh/Scottish/Northern Irish, Irish, Other European (grouped as White for the purposes of this analysis), West Indian or Guyanese (grouped as Black), Indian (as is), Pakistani, Bangladeshi (grouped as Pakistani or Bangladeshi), Mixed parentage or any other ethnic group (grouped as Other).

Figure 3.1: Young people's educational aspirations and parental education

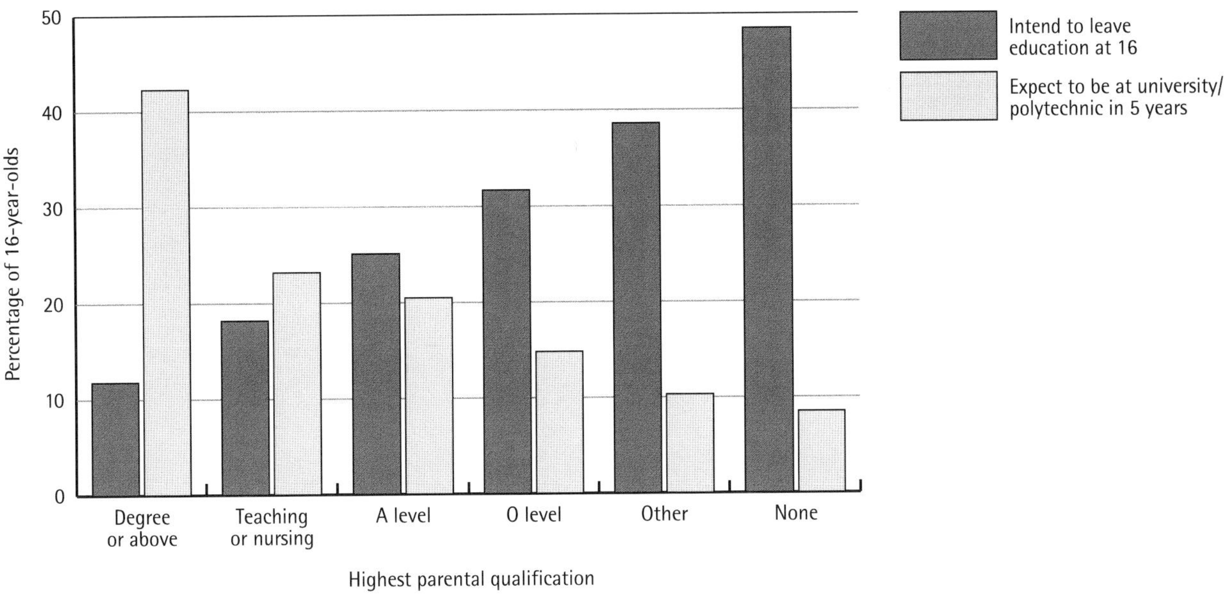

Source: BCS70 age 16 survey

Multivariate analysis

The bullet points and figure above have picked out some characteristics that may be of particular interest or importance in explaining the variation in aspirations among young people. But as indicated by the overview in the first part of Chapter 2, there is a very wide range of factors which sociological, psychological and economic theory predict will be relevant, and for which previous research has found some support. Moreover, these factors are in some cases associated with each other – people from a lower social-class background are likely to have achieved less academic success to date, for example.

Table 3.1 summarises the results from multivariate regressions, taking into account as many of these factors as possible for which there are indicators in the data. The first column lists the factors, the second column shows their independent association with an aspiration to leave education at 16 (logit regression), and the third column shows their independent association with lower occupational aspirations (based on occupational social class; ordered logit regression).

The first point to note is that being disabled is associated with a slightly lower likelihood of intending to leave education at 16, after controlling for other characteristics, while there is

no statistically significant difference in the level of occupational aspirations between disabled and non-disabled young people. These results confirm that young disabled people's aspirations are certainly no lower in these two important respects than their non-disabled counterparts.[18]

Sub-groups among the disabled young people were also investigated in a multivariate framework (those with mental health problems, more severe impairments, or who became disabled later in childhood) but none of these characteristics was consistently significant statistically. This may be because the numbers in the sample are too small.

Personal characteristics that come through as significantly and independently associated with higher aspirations are being from an Indian or a Pakistani or Bangladeshi background, having higher self-esteem or a stronger sense of being able to determine your own fate, and having a positive attitude towards school and schoolwork.

18 This regression looks at staying on in education, regardless of what the young person is staying on to do, and without consideration of what the alternatives might be. The previous chapter indicated that disabled young people who stay on may be more likely to follow secondary and vocational courses rather than further or higher education.

Table 3.1: Multivariate regressions on young people's aspirations at age 16

Characteristics	Intend to leave education at 16		Aspire to lower-status occupation	
	Coefficient[a]	Significance[b]	Coefficient[a]	Significance[b]
Personal				
Disability status:				
Non-disabled	Reference		Reference	
Uncertain	0.179	ns	0.115	ns
Disabled	−0.517	*	−0.301	ns
Gender:				
Female	Reference		Reference	
Male	0.296	***	0.214	***
Ethnicity:				
White	Reference		Reference	
Black	−1.126	**	−0.331	ns
Indian	−1.581	***	−0.742	***
Pakistani/Bangladeshi	−1.028	**	−1.135	***
Other	−0.818	*	−0.556	*
Higher self-esteem	−0.069	***		
Internal locus of control			−0.011	***
Positive attitude to school	−0.127	***	−0.071	***
Parental				
Aspirations for teenager:				
HE	−1.635	***	−0.687	***
FE	−2.708	***	−1.011	***
Vocational training	−1.933	***	−0.098	ns
Leave	Reference		Reference	
Other	−0.806	***	−0.165	ns
Don't know	−0.063	ns	0.372	ns
Highest parental qualifications:				
Degree	Reference		Reference	
Teaching/nursing	0.221	ns	0.646	***
A level	0.203	ns	0.433	***
O level	0.502	***	0.542	***
Other	0.719	***	0.676	***
None	1.009	***	0.661	***
Parental social class:				
I/II	Reference		Reference	
I/II and lower	0.452	***	0.058	ns
III manual/non-manual	0.605	***	0.264	***
III and lower	0.591	***	0.337	***
IV/V	0.888	***	0.235	*
Other	0.505	***	0.260	**
Experience				
Teacher gives poor assessment of academic performance	0.446	***	0.362	***
Work experience:				
Useful	Reference		Reference	
Maybe useful	0.210	ns	0.085	ns
Not useful	−0.055	ns	−0.037	ns
None	−0.178	*	−0.155	**
Has boy/girlfriend:				
Yes, now	Reference			
Yes, before	−0.160	*		
No	−0.452	***		
School				
Specialist help given:				
No	Reference			
Yes	−0.500	*		
Type of school:				
Mainstream	Reference		Reference	
Special	0.081	ns	−0.558	ns
Other	0.734	***	0.324	***
Constant/cut points	Y		Y	
Number of respondents	*4,921*		*4,813*	
Percentage of cases correctly classified by regression model	*79.8*		*36.7*	

Notes:
[a] If coefficient column left blank, variable not included in this regression; [b] Significance: ns = not significant; * = 90%; ** = 95%, *** = 99% or higher.
Source: BCS70 age 16 survey

Parental background characteristics are among the most important: parental aspirations, their own education and their (combined) social class are all significant influences on their teenagers' educational and occupational aspirations.

The teachers' assessment of the young person's academic potential is also important; other school-related variables less so. Attending a special school – having controlled for other characteristics including disability – is not significantly associated with higher or lower aspirations (although the lack of significance may be due to the small numbers involved).[19] Having work experience is associated with a lower likelihood of wanting to stay on in education; in fact the causation probably goes the other way in this case – those who want to leave school at 16 are more likely to be offered and take up work experience.

Differences in the influences on disabled and non-disabled young people's aspirations

Overall, the differences between disabled and non-disabled young people's aspirations are small but that does not necessarily imply that the influences on the formation of aspirations for the two groups are the same. It could be that parental background, for example, is more important for disabled young people than it is for non-disabled young people. This section addresses that question, by looking for statistically significant interactions between disability and each of the other characteristics listed in Table 3.1.

- Gender
  Non-disabled boys are the most likely to want to leave education, followed by girls (whether or not they are disabled), with disabled boys the least likely to be intending to leave.

- Personal attitudes
  Having an 'internal locus of control' (that is, having a stronger belief in your ability to determine your own fate) is even more important for disabled young people than it is

for non-disabled youngsters in forming high occupational aspirations. Similarly, having a positive attitude to school and school work is more strongly associated with higher occupational aspirations for disabled teenagers than it is for non-disabled young people.

- Parental aspirations
  While the association between parental aspirations and non-disabled teenagers' educational aspirations is strong, it is much weaker for disabled young people. However, when it comes to occupational aspirations, the parents' influence on disabled youngsters appears to be slightly stronger than it is for non-disabled young people.

- Parental qualifications
  The association between parental qualifications and disabled teenagers' educational aspirations is stronger than it is for non-disabled young people. With respect to occupational aspirations, there is no significant difference by disability status.

- Teachers' assessment of academic ability
  Teachers' assessments of academic ability seem to make more difference to disabled young people's occupational aspirations than is the case for non-disabled young people, although it is significant for both groups.

- Having a boy/girlfriend
  Both disabled and non-disabled young people who have a boy/girlfriend are more likely to want to leave education at 16. This could be an indication that their interests lie elsewhere, or that they are keen to assert their independence. In any case, the association between boy/girlfriend status and educational aspirations is much stronger for disabled young people.

Summary

This chapter has explored the influences on young people's educational and occupational aspirations. As illustrated by the pen pictures drawn from the data at the beginning of the chapter, each individual's circumstances are unique and the range and interplay between different factors is highly complex. The process is anything but deterministic.

---

[19] The 'other' category is mostly boarding schools (not including residential special schools) and other children living away from home.

Attempting to draw any generalisations on such a topic is difficult, but some patterns do emerge. Although there are too few individuals in the survey to draw statistically robust conclusions about variation in aspirations by type and severity of impairment, the results suggest that young people with mental health problems, those with more severe impairments or more complex needs, and those who became disabled later in childhood, are all likely to have lower aspirations than other disabled young people.

There is a strong gradient in educational and occupational aspirations of young people with respect to their parents' educational and social-class background. Young people who have parents neither of whom have any educational qualifications are more than four times as likely to intend to leave education at 16 than young people who have at least one parent educated to degree level.

On the whole, it seems that parents are a stronger influence on disabled young people than on non-disabled young people. The evidence is somewhat mixed here, with the association between parental aspirations and teenagers' intentions to leave education being weaker for disabled young people than others. This could reflect the delicate balance referred to in the literature reviewed at the beginning of the previous chapter, between the importance of parental support for disabled young people on the one hand, and their occasional tendency to underestimate their youngster's capabilities on the other.

Aside from external influences, the young person's own motivation and outlook is also crucial. This appears to be especially the case for disabled young people: those with a firmer belief in their ability to shape their future are more likely to aim high.

The next two chapters take up the story in early adulthood, where we can observe to what extent these educational and occupational aspirations are translated into reality.

4

Educational outcomes and transition to early adult life

The previous two chapters have examined young people's aspirations and the influences on them. The stories of Dan and Janine, drawn from the 1970 British Cohort Study (BCS70), were introduced to illustrate the contrasting circumstances of 16-year-olds. This chapter begins by taking forward those stories into early adulthood. It then provides some background on the nature of transition for young people in general and disabled people in particular, before presenting results from quantitative analysis of the Youth Cohort Studies (YCS) and BCS70 on the educational attainment of disabled and non-disabled young adults. For each group, the relationships between attainment, aspirations and other influences are examined. Chapter 5 undertakes a similar analysis with respect to employment outcomes.

The stories continue

Boxes 4.1 and 4.2 continue the account of Dan and Janine's lives up to the of age 26, where we see how their aspirations have panned out in early adult life. As before, all information is drawn from the responses given by the two individuals to questions in the survey, but of course the names are fictional.

There are many aspects of Dan's and Janine's situations that could explain the divergence in their experience and the contrast between Dan's fulfilment of his aspirations and Janine's disappointment. It could be related to their impairments, to their education, to their parental background, their personal motivation or any combination of these and other factors. The process of transition is complex.

Box 4.1: Dan's story

At age 16, Dan was aiming high: he wanted to go on to higher education and to become a bank manager. He had a sight impairment and some mental health problems, and was not entirely happy either at school or at home.

By age 26, he is part way through a professional accounting qualification, having achieved eight O levels, two CSE grade 1s, four A levels and a degree.

He works full time as an accounts clerk in a large firm. He has worked with the same employer for five years and he earns £208 per week take-home pay (just slightly above the average for all employees in the sample). He is fortunate enough never to have been unemployed since leaving college.

He is buying a house with a mortgage and is cohabiting with his girlfriend who is also working full-time. They do not have any children as yet.

His life satisfaction is slightly below the median for his peers, but his malaise score – a general indicator of mental well-being – is on the median. He feels he does have choices and control in his life, and thinks his standard of living is 'the same' as others of his own age.

Box 4.2: Janine's story

At age 16, Janine was attending a special school. She wanted to stay on in education and train to become a teacher or for some other professional occupation. She has spina bifida.

In the event, she left school at 17 with no qualifications although she subsequently acquired an NVQ level 1. She is currently on a training scheme, and has been on two Youth Training Schemes before. She has never had a full-time or part-time job.

She lives with her parents and is single. She believes her standard of living is 'a bit better' than other people of her age, perhaps because she is living with her parents.

She rates her life satisfaction at 6 on a scale of 0 to 10, which is slightly below the average for her age group, and she feels she does usually have choice and control over her life. However, her malaise score is 10, which is in the lowest tenth of the whole sample.

Changing nature of transition

In a review for the Joseph Rowntree Foundation, Meadows (2001) concluded that the pathways from youth to adulthood have become much more varied in recent decades. This is confirmed by Bynner et al (2002) in their study comparing the 1958 birth cohort (the National Child Development Survey, NCDS) with the 1970 birth cohort (BCS70). They found that staying-on rates in education rose through the 1980s and 1990s for both 16- to 17-year-olds and 18- to 24-year-olds. The percentage of 18-year-olds gaining two or more A levels (the standard minimum entry requirement for higher education) has also risen from 1986 onwards, having been flat for the previous decade. However, for those who do leave school at the end of compulsory education, employment has become more marginalised: where previously 15- and 16-year-olds had been able to enter craft apprenticeships and secretarial work, now they are more likely to enter sales and service sector occupations, often part-time, poorly paid and with limited prospects. Employment prospects are more strongly influenced by educational qualifications for the 1970 cohort than for the 1958 cohort. Similarly, the penalty associated with childhood poverty, in terms of educational qualifications, risk of unemployment, and low earnings in adulthood, increased between the two cohorts.

Differences in employment between men and women in early adulthood have narrowed (Ferri et al, 2003). Their employment rates, earnings and occupations have converged, although significant differences still remain, especially among those with lower educational qualifications. This is partly because those with less education are more likely to make 'accelerated transitions': from school into work, and into starting a family. Both these transitions tend to increase the differences between men and women.

Experiences of young disabled adults

A small number of studies have looked at education and employment outcomes in early adulthood specifically for disabled people. Using the NCDS, Pilling (1995) found that disabled people were doing less well in terms of employment and earnings by age 23 than their non-disabled counterparts. Those with mental health problems, more severe impairments, and those who were disabled at birth were especially disadvantaged.

A follow-up study to the 1985 Office of Population Censuses and Surveys (OPCS) surveys of disability found that disabled young people were less likely to be living independently, less likely to have work experience, more likely to be unemployed, and if they were in work, they were earning less, on average, than non-disabled people of the same age (Hirst and Baldwin, 1994). Differences between younger disabled and non-disabled adults are smaller than for older disabled and non-disabled adults, suggesting they drift apart as opportunities for gaining independence diminish.

Similar findings were produced by a follow-up of 274 disabled young people aged 15 to 21 who had been beneficiaries of the Joseph Rowntree

Memorial Trust Family Fund (Hirst, 1987). Few of the physically disabled young people obtained steady employment and those who did were mostly in junior clerical roles or other low-grade non-manual jobs. There was little alternative provision to paid employment, so those who were not in work were often 'doing nothing'. Hirst concluded that the association between socioeconomic disadvantage and disability compounded the difficulties of transition for these young people.

The critical role of educational qualifications is again highlighted by these studies. Disabled young people who do succeed in gaining educational qualifications are much more likely to secure independence and employment in early adult life than those who leave school without qualifications (Hirst 1987; Hendey and Pascall, 2001).

According to higher education statistics, the proportion of students at university who are recorded as disabled has been gradually rising (HESA, 2004). However, their experience is not always smooth: most disabled students experience barriers including the physical environment (which also affects their choice of course and institution), adjustments that are agreed in principle but not implemented in practice, and lecturers who are reluctant to make adjustments for fear that doing so would provide an 'unfair' advantage (Fuller et al, 2004; Tinklin et al, 2004).

Four of the young people interviewed for this study had experience of higher education, and they gave mixed reports. One woman had had to give up her first attempt at a degree because the campus was 'irremediably inaccessible'. Two had spent time campaigning to improve the disability services on offer – of considerable benefit to later generations of students, and potentially useful experience, but nevertheless a distraction from studying. Three of the four mentioned aspects of their courses that were inaccessible, often as a result of inflexibility in modes of teaching or examination. On the other hand, all four had enjoyed their time at university overall. In addition to academic development, they particularly valued opportunities for work placements, and getting involved in clubs and societies.

Experience following compulsory education

Outcomes at age 16/17

The first new quantitative evidence presented here on the experiences of disabled and non-disabled young people after the end of compulsory schooling comes from the Youth Cohort Studies (YCS) conducted at age 16/17 (cohorts 9 and 10, in 1998 and 2000). Table 4.1 shows what disabled and non-disabled people were doing at the time of the survey and gives an indication of the experience of 'transition' so

Table 4.1: Current activity and experience since last year[a]

	Non-disabled		Disabled	
	Current activity (column %)	of whom, % who got what they wanted	Current activity (column %)	of whom, % who got what they wanted
Full-time education	71	71	61	60
Full-time job	9	36	9	39
Part-time job	2	19	4	27
Training[b]	11	65	14	55
Something else	2	24	4	16
Out of work	5	10	9	22
Total	100	62	100	52
Number of respondents	26,612		1,160	

Notes:

[a] Results weighted using weights supplied with the data.

[b] Government-sponsored training, including Modern Apprenticeships.

Source: YCS cohort 9 sweep 1 and cohort 10 sweep 1

far. Disabled young people are less likely to be continuing in education and are more likely to be out of work or doing 'something else' (including part-time education or looking after the family). Moreover, while three fifths of non-disabled people report that they got the education or training place, or job, that they wanted, only just over half of disabled youngsters say the same.

In addition, disabled young people are more likely to assess the process of transition from school to their current activity as 'very difficult' or 'difficult', and the difference between disabled and non-disabled young people in this respect is statistically significant.

Outcomes at age 18/19

These same respondents were followed up two years later, at age 18/19 (sweep 3 of cohorts 9 and 10, in the years 2000 and 2002 respectively). At this sweep, just over 4% of the sample reported a "health problem or disability, that you might expect will last for more than a year, which affects your ability to carry out normal day to day activities". This corresponds to 423 individuals, out of a total sample size of 13,489.

Figure 4.1 shows the main activity reported by the young adults at the time of the survey. Non-disabled young adults are more likely than disabled young adults to still be in full-time education (41% compared to 36%), and they are also more likely to be in full-time work (32% compared to 23%). Conversely, disabled 18/19-year-olds are nearly three times as likely as non-disabled adults of the same age to be unemployed or 'doing something else' (25% compared to 9%). This indicates a widening gap between disabled and non-disabled unemployment rates since the age of 16/17.

One of the crucial ways in which young adults of this age may be equipped for their future is through the educational qualifications they have obtained. Table 4.2 shows the highest qualification achieved to date for each group. Non-disabled young adults are nearly twice as likely to have obtained A levels than their disabled counterparts, and, conversely, just under half of all disabled young people have their highest qualification at level 1 or below – that is, lower than GCSE grade C or equivalent – a much higher proportion than non-disabled young people.

Figure 4.1: Main activity at age 18/19

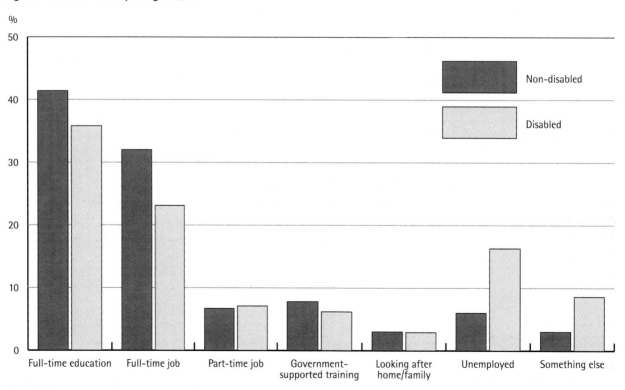

Note: Weighted results using weights supplied with the data.
Source: YCS cohort 9 sweep 3 and cohort 10 sweep 3

Table 4.2: Highest educational qualification obtained (%)

	Non-disabled	Disabled
Level 3 academic (A levels)	30.7	16.4
Level 3 vocational or mixed	9.9	6.5
Level 2 academic (GCSE grade A*-C)	13.7	11.4
Level 2 vocational or mixed	17.6	17.6
Level 1 or below (GCSE grades D-G)	28.1	48.2
Total	100.0	100.0
Number of respondents (unweighted)	12,972	423

Note: Weighted results using weights supplied with the data.

Source: YCS cohort 9 sweep 3 and cohort 10 sweep 3

It could be that some disabled young people spend longer acquiring qualifications, due to periods of ill health or medical intervention, or because of barriers in accessing the educational opportunities they want. For this reason it is interesting to look at what qualifications those who are still in education are aiming to achieve. Table 4.3 indicates that it is indeed the case that a higher proportion of disabled young people still in education are taking A and AS level courses than the proportion of non-disabled young people (although as Figure 4.1 shows, the overall percentage of disabled people still in education is lower). However, even if all of those individuals succeeded in obtaining their A levels and went on into higher education, that would not be enough to close the gap between the proportion of disabled and non-disabled young adults studying for a degree. A surprisingly high

Table 4.3: Qualification aim in current study (%)

	Non-disabled	Disabled
Degree	42.5	23.3
Other higher education	6.1	6.7
A/AS level	8.9	15.7
Other level 3 qualification	20.3	19.7
GCSE	1.0	1.8
Other level 2 qualification	9.9	17.4
Level 1 or other qualification	4.5	7.9
Not specified	6.9	7.5
Total	100.0	100.0
Number of respondents (unweighted)	7,993	236

Note: Weighted results using weights supplied with the data.
Source: YCS cohort 9 sweep 3 and cohort 10 sweep 3

proportion of disabled 18/19-year-olds are taking level 2 vocational courses.[20]

These differences are confirmed by looking at the location of study. Forty-three per cent of disabled adults who are studying full time or part time are at school, sixth-form college or a college of further education, compared to 28% of non-disabled people at this age. Conversely, a higher proportion of non-disabled young people are attending a higher education institute at this age.

Outcomes at age 26

We turn now to the BCS70, for information on young people a little further into their adult lives, at age 26. These data were collected in 1996, in other words, a few years before the data on 18/19-year-olds reported above. This analysis uses a four-way classification of disability status, reflecting the fact that some cohort members become disabled between the ages of 16 and 26, and some who were disabled at age 16 no longer report disability at age 26. The details of this classification, including discussion of measurement error, are given in the Appendix.

Young people disabled at both ages are much more likely than other groups to have obtained no educational qualifications by 26 (Table 4.4). This difference is statistically significant at the 95% level.

These results do not take account of the problem of non-random attrition; that is, the characteristics of those who dropped out of the survey between ages 16 and 26 are not a representative cross-section of the whole sample (see Box 1.1 in Chapter 1, p 3). A simple regression reveals that young people disabled at both ages 16 and 26 are significantly less likely to achieve higher educational qualifications than their non-disabled counterparts from the same background, and that there is a strong effect of parental educational

---

[20] Wage premia from vocational qualifications are typically lower than for academic qualifications (Dearden et al, 2002). However, the value of vocational qualifications measured in this way is higher for low-ability individuals than for higher-ability individuals, so they clearly have a role to play.

qualifications on qualifications obtained by the young person.[21]

Fulfilment of educational aspirations?

Comparing the educational aspirations expressed at 16 with qualifications obtained by age 26, the first point to note is the strength of the association between aspiration and outcome (Figure 4.2). This is perhaps not surprising since by age 16, many young people will already have decided whether to stay on in education, and that in turn has major implications for their future trajectory.

Table 4.4: Highest qualification obtained by age 26 (%)

Highest qualification obtained	Disabled at neither age	Disabled at 16, not 26	Became disabled	Disabled at both ages
No qualifications	4.0	6.1	4.0	8.0
CSE level 2–5/NVQ level 1	16.1	19.0	16.0	18.0
O level/NVQ level 2	41.1	38.5	42.9	40.0
A level/NVQ level 3	11.9	8.9	12.1	7.0
Higher qualification/NVQ level 4	4.8	4.1	4.8	5.0
Degree/NVQ level 5 or 6	22.1	23.5	20.2	22.0
Total	100.0	100.0	100.0	100.0
Number of respondents	*4,210*	*247*	*769*	*100*

Source: BCS70 age 26 survey

Figure 4.2: Highest qualification at age 26 by aspiration at age 16

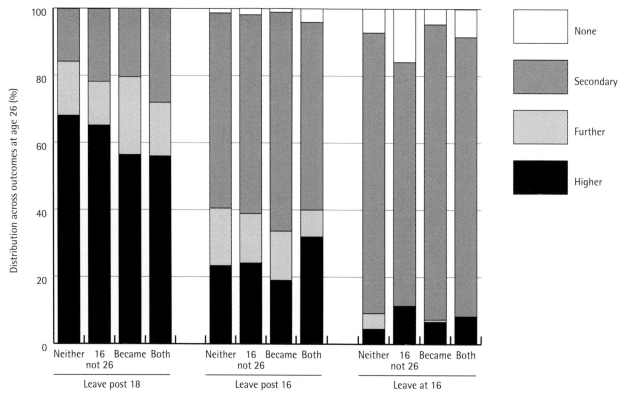

Source: BCS70 age 16 and age 26 surveys

---

[21] Ordered logit regression on highest educational qualification, with dummies for disability status and for parental education. Details available from the author on request.

Among those who already at 16 thought they would continue in education after the age of 18 (in other words, those who were aiming for higher education of some kind), the majority did indeed obtain a degree. However, the proportion of the non-disabled who did so is greater than those who either became disabled between the ages of 16 and 26 or were disabled at both ages.

On the other hand, among those who were intending to stay on at 16 but not necessarily at 18, a higher proportion of those who were disabled at both ages, compared to other groups, exceeded their earlier aspiration and in fact got a degree.

Collapsing the categories into 'exceeded', 'met' or 'fell below' educational aspirations, young people disabled at both ages are more likely to do less well than they had hoped, compared to the other groups. Two fifths (41%) fell below their initial level of aspiration compared to 35% of young people disabled at neither age.[22]

Influences on the chances of fulfilment

Aspirations are one important influence on outcomes, but there are also direct influences from parental background and personal characteristics. Table 4.5 explores the relationship between educational attainment and disability, controlling for level of aspiration and parental background. The results confirm that both educational aspirations and parental background are significantly associated with attainment. It also shows that young people who become disabled between the ages of 16 and 26 are at a disadvantage in attainment relative to their aspirations. This is perhaps to be expected: a major life event has intervened between the time at which aspirations are formed and the time at which attainment is being measured. More striking is the fact that young people who are disabled at both ages 16 and 26 are also less likely to attain high educational qualifications. As we saw in Chapters 2 and 3, the aspirations of

these young people at age 16 were comparable to their non-disabled peers, but their educational outcomes relative to their aspirations are lower.

To test whether parental background has a similar effect on attainment for young people regardless of their disability status, a second analysis was performed with an 'interaction term' between parental education and disability status. The results showed no consistent pattern; it appears that having well-educated parents is no more or less important for disabled young people's outcomes than for non-disabled young people.

In general it is also the case that educational aspirations do not matter more or less to outcomes for disabled people than for disabled people. The exception is those who become disabled between the ages of 16 and 26, for whom aspirations are less closely linked to outcomes.

Among disabled young people, those with a more severe impairment or several impairments, and those who became disabled later in childhood are less likely to attain higher educational qualifications. Taking disabled and non-disabled young people together, the following are independently and significantly associated with higher educational attainment, for a given level of aspiration and controlling for the characteristics listed in Table 4.5:

- being male;
- being Pakistani or Bangladeshi, followed by being White, Indian or Other (ie being from a Black ethnic background is a disadvantage);
- having an internal locus of control;
- being from a higher parental social-class background;
- receiving a better assessment by the teacher of academic ability at age 16.

---

[22] This difference is statistically significant at the 90% level. The classification counts all those whose aspiration was to leave at 16 as having met or exceeded their aspiration, whether they obtained any qualifications or not.

Table 4.5: Educational attainment controlling for aspirations, disability status and parental education: ordered logit regression on highest qualification attained by age 26

	Coefficient	Significance[a]
Aspiration at 16:		
University/polytechnic	Reference	
Teaching; technical or art college	-1.625	***
Post-18 not otherwise specified	-1.889	***
A level	-1.434	***
Post-16 vocational	-3.551	***
Post-16 O level/CSE	-3.196	***
Post-16 not otherwise specified	-2.545	***
Leave at 16: job	-4.137	***
Leave at 16: other	-4.287	***
Parental highest qualification:		
Degree or higher	Reference	
Teaching, nursing	-0.504	***
A level	-0.485	***
O level	-0.920	***
Other	-0.842	***
None	-1.382	***
Disability status:		
Disabled at neither age	Reference	
Recovered	-0.268	ns
Became disabled	-0.275	***
Disabled at both ages	-0.616	**
Number of respondents		2,888
Percentage of cases correctly classified by regression model		55.3

Notes:
[a] Significance: ns = not significant; * = 90%; ** = 95%; *** = 99% or higher.
Source: BCS70 age 16 and age 26 surveys

Summary

The main findings of this chapter are as follows:

• Immediately following the end of compulsory schooling, around half of disabled young people are doing what they wanted to be doing, compared to around three fifths of non-disabled young people. Disabled young people are more than twice as likely to be out of work or doing 'something else' than non-disabled young people.
• At age 18/19, disabled young people are less likely to be in full-time education than non-disabled people of the same age. Those who are studying are more likely to be pursuing secondary-level or vocational qualifications.
• There appears to be some improvement in educational qualifications for disabled people between the ages of 18/19 and 26 (although

strictly speaking the two surveys are not directly comparable: they use different definitions of disability and refer to different cohorts). However, taking account of non-random attrition from the age 26 survey, reveals that the qualifications of disabled young adults are considerably lower than those of non-disabled people of the same age.
• Aspirations are an important, independent, influence on educational outcomes, for disabled and non-disabled young people alike.
• Controlling for other characteristics, young people who become disabled between the ages of 16 and 26, and those who are disabled at both ages, have lower educational attainment relative to their aspirations than do their non-disabled counterparts.

The previous chapters showed that the aspirations of disabled teenagers were comparable in scope and ambition to those of non-disabled teenagers, although their expectations were more muted. This chapter has indicated that their educational attainment, both in absolute terms and relative to their aspirations, is more limited. Other research has consistently demonstrated the importance of educational attainment in shaping adult life, especially in terms of the chances of employment and quality of employment that the individual can expect. The next chapter examines those outcomes in detail.

5

Occupational outcomes: fulfilment and frustration

This chapter examines the labour market experience of disabled and non-disabled people in early adulthood. The role of aspirations, prior educational achievement and other background characteristics are considered. In addition, changes in the subjective well-being of young adults are described, which offer an insight into the psychological impact of the process of transition for different groups.

Influences on occupational outcomes

Aspirations and education

It is generally accepted that both aspirations and educational attainment are important influences on occupational outcomes. In a study focusing on aspirations among 16-year-olds to become scientists, self-assessed ability, maths test scores, various aspects of personality, social background and gender were all important predictors of attainment by age 33, in addition to aspirations at 16 (Schoon, 2001). On the other hand, occupational aspirations in teenage years tend to outstrip later achievements, on average (Maziels, 1970): there is a general process of downwards adjustment. Moreover, the gradient in aspirations by social-class background observed among teenagers translates into an even steeper gradient by social class in employment and occupation in early adulthood (Furlong, 1992).

More generally, educational attainment, parental social class, material conditions during childhood, and parental aspirations have been found to be important predictors of outcomes in early adulthood (O'Brien and Jones, 1999; Schoon and Parsons, 2002). It is not just

conditions at a particular point in time but cumulative disadvantage over the lifetime which matter (Schoon et al, 2002).

Once again, however, it is important to remember that these conclusions are based on averages and tendencies, rather than deterministic processes. Pilling (1990) focused on those who 'escaped from disadvantage' in the National Child Development Study, and found the chances of escape were influenced by the extent and duration of socioeconomic disadvantage in childhood, family type and stress, parental involvement in education, locality, and the aspirations and motivation of the young person themselves.

Disability

In a survey of 16- to 24-year-olds for the Disability Rights Commission, 13% said they had been turned down for a paid job and told it was due to disability, and a further 18% had suspected that the rejection of their application was due to disability (Wilson, 2003).

One of the young people interviewed for this study had a full-time job, one had a part-time job and two were on work placements. All of them had concerns about their future employment. Problems that had already been experienced included: rejection by a prospective employer on grounds of health and safety, lack of Deaf awareness on the part of training providers, delays in adaptations to work premises (resulting in a postponement of the start-date of the job), and lack of part-time opportunities. One interviewee had concluded that her future lay in working for Deaf organisations because other employers were insufficiently well-organised to

Figure 5.1: Distribution by bands of hourly pay

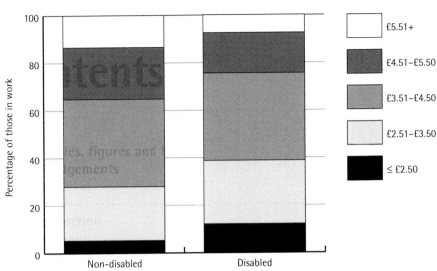

Note: Weighted results using weights supplied with the data.
Source: YCS cohort 9 sweep 3 and cohort 10 sweep 3

enable her to realise her potential. Another had recognised that she would need a flexible manager and a job where she could work from home for at least part of the time, and she was concerned that such opportunities might be in short supply.

Occupational outcomes at age 18/19

In the Youth Cohort Study (YCS), two thirds of non-disabled 18/19-year-olds and half of disabled respondents said that they had some paid work in the week prior to the survey. This may have been alongside education or other activities, and was not necessarily their main activity. Disabled and non-disabled young people in employment work similar hours: 32.5 on average, with no statistically significant difference between the two groups. However, their remuneration does differ: an average of £135 per week for the non-disabled and £125 per week for the disabled. This difference is statistically significant at the 95% level. Translating that into hourly pay, Figure 5.1 shows the distribution of disabled and non-disabled employees.[23]

Disabled employees are more than twice as likely to be reporting hourly wages of £2.50 per hour or less and are also more likely to have wages

between £2.51 and £3.50. This cannot be directly assigned to discrimination since, as we have seen, disabled young people bring lower formal qualifications to the labour market than non-disabled young people, and the two groups of workers may be in different kinds of jobs. However, a regression of hourly pay on occupational group, educational qualifications and disability status, shows that being disabled is independently associated with significantly lower wages.[24] These simple results are indicative of differential treatment of disabled workers, although there are other factors one would wish to take into account (not available in the dataset) before drawing firm conclusions.

Figure 5.2 shows that the distribution of disabled and non-disabled workers across major occupational groups at this age are similar. These are broad groups and there could still be differences within groups in the kinds of jobs disabled and non-disabled young people undertake.

One quarter (25%) of disabled respondents and 11% of non-disabled respondents are not in education, employment or training. Respondents in this situation are asked to identify which of a list of possible reasons applies to them. Some of these are positive, for example, 'having a break from study', or 'looking after the home or

---

[23] There is always measurement error in wages and hours of work. However, there is no reason to believe that the error will be systematic or that its effects will differ between disability sub-groups.

[24] Ordinary least squares regression on hourly pay. Coefficient on 'being disabled' is –0.358, significant at the 90% level.

Figure 5.2: Distribution across occupational groups

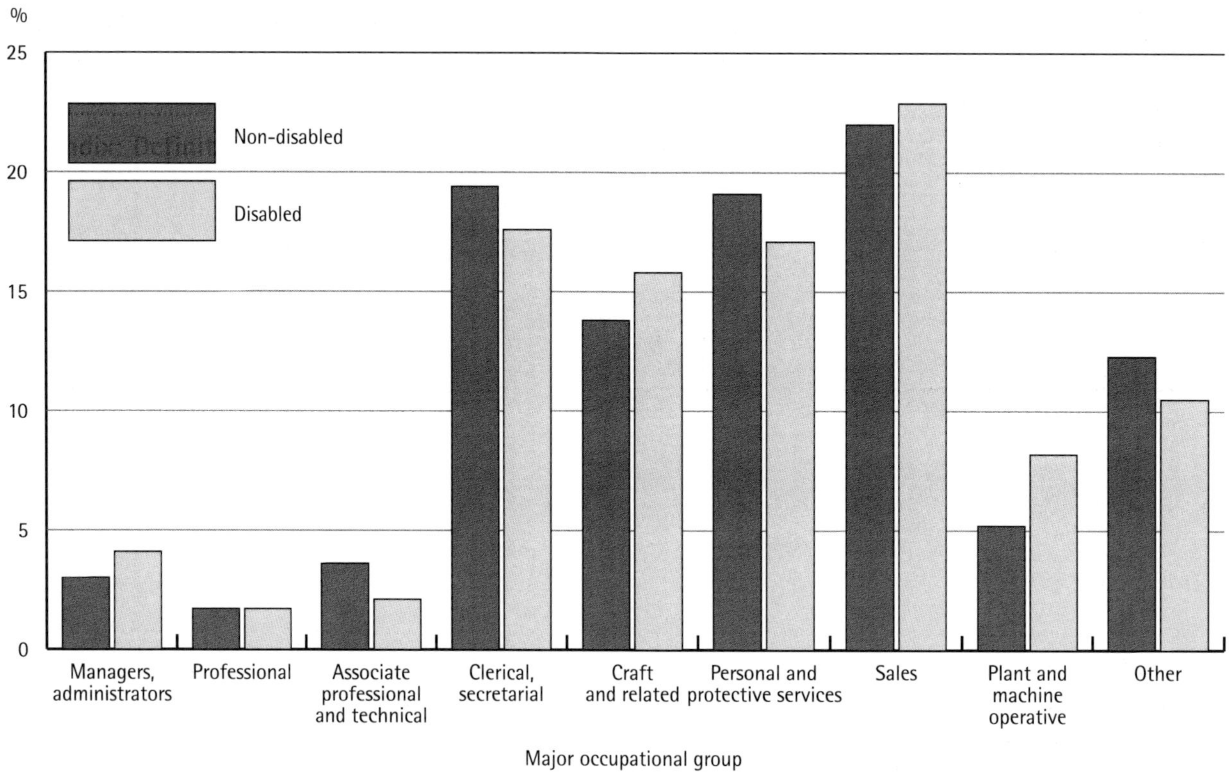

Note: Weighted results using weights supplied with the data.
Source: YCS cohort 9 sweep 3 and cohort 10 sweep 3

children', and others are negative, for example, 'housing problems', or 'family problems'.[25] If the negative reasons are balanced against the positive, the overall average is slightly negative (–1.0), but more strongly so for disabled respondents than for non-disabled respondents (–1.6 compared to –0.9; difference statistically significant at the 99% level).

The survey also collects information about activity over the last calendar year (1999 in the case of cohort 9 and 2001 in the case of cohort 10). The majority of both disabled and non-disabled young adults have avoided unemployment during the year, but 22% of the former and 14% of the latter have not (a

statistically significant difference). Among these, two fifths of the non-disabled young people were unemployed for three months or less. The disabled young adults were much more likely to have an extended period of unemployment: nearly one in three was unemployed for the whole 12 months, compared to just one in 20 of the non-disabled group.

Not surprisingly, the combined effect of lower educational achievement, higher rates of unemployment and worse rates of pay mean that disabled 18/19-year-olds have a dimmer view of the future than their non-disabled counterparts. A list of five statements about attitudes towards the future, some positive and some negative, reveals that disabled respondents are more likely to feel that things have not gone well for them since the age of 16, that they are not well-equipped to find out about opportunities, that they lack qualifications they need and that making plans is a waste of time. Combining these items into a score, their outlook overall at this age is significantly less positive, on average, than the outlook of non-disabled youngsters.

---

[25] For cohort 9 the positive reasons are: having a break from study, looking after home/children, looking after other relatives. The negative reasons are: need more qualifications, poor health/disability, housing problems, family problems, transport difficulties, would be financially worse off, there are no decent opportunities, not yet decided what to do, drug/alcohol problems, and criminal record. For cohort 10, an additional two positive reasons are listed: just finished exams, and waiting to take up a placement or job; and one additional negative reason: not found a suitable place.

Table 5.1: Labour market status at age 26 (%)

	Disabled at neither age	Disabled at 16, not 26	Became disabled between ages 16 and 26	Disabled at both ages
Full-time employed or self-employed	77.6	76.0	67.3	61.5
Part-time employed or self-employed	7.8	9.7	8.7	12.9
Full-time education or training	2.6	3.9	4.2	5.5
Looking after home or family	7.9	6.2	7.0	4.6
Unemployed, sick/disabled	3.7	3.9	12.2	13.8
Other	0.5	0.4	0.6	1.8
Total	100.0	100.0	100.0	100.0
Number of respondents	*4,393*	*258*	*808*	*107*

Source: BCS70 age 26 survey

Occupational outcomes at age 26

Employment status

Table 5.1 shows the labour market status of respondents at the age of 26. Those who were disabled at neither 16 nor 26, and those who were disabled but no longer reporting disability are most likely to be in full-time employment. Young people disabled at both ages are more likely than other groups to be in part-time employment, but the addition is not sufficient to close the gap in the proportion in employment overall: 89% of those disabled at neither age and 74% of those disabled at both ages.

Conversely, disabled 26-year-olds who were also disabled at 16 are nearly four times more likely to be unemployed or 'sick/disabled' (ie not working) than young people who were disabled at neither age. Cumulatively, the difference between these two groups is statistically significant at the 99% level.

It is interesting that those who have become disabled since age 16 show greater resemblance in this instance to the 'disabled at both ages' group than to the disabled at neither age, whereas in the corresponding table in the previous chapter (Table 4.4) on educational attainment, this was not the case. The attainment (or non-attainment) of educational qualifications is likely to be affected by experience at school at younger ages – prior to the onset of disability for this group – whereas labour market activity is affected by contemporary circumstances as well as previous experience.

Occupation

Of those in work, the distribution across occupational social class is shown in Figure 5.3. Only slightly lower proportions of people disabled at both ages 16 and 26 are in professional and managerial/technical occupations than those disabled at neither age. On the other hand, twice the proportion of people disabled at both ages are in partly skilled or unskilled jobs (30%, compared to 15% of those disabled at neither age). The cumulative difference in occupational social class between these two groups is statistically significant at the 95% level.

Once again, however, it is important to take account of the possible effect of attrition bias on these results. A simple regression on occupational class, controlling for parental social-class background, shows that the parents' social class has a strong association with the occupations of their offspring at age 26.[26] The regression also shows that for a given parental background, disabled young people are significantly less likely to be working in high-status occupations than their non-disabled counterparts. This is the case even though there is strong selection into employment (that is, many more disabled young people are not in work at all). Comparing with the results for 18/19-year-olds reported above (Figure 5.2), this could indicate that the distribution across occupations of disabled and non-disabled people diverges as they get older (although it is also consistent with there being a difference between the 1970 birth cohort and the later cohorts).

---

[26] Details available from the author on request.

Figure 5.3: Occupational social class (based on current employment)

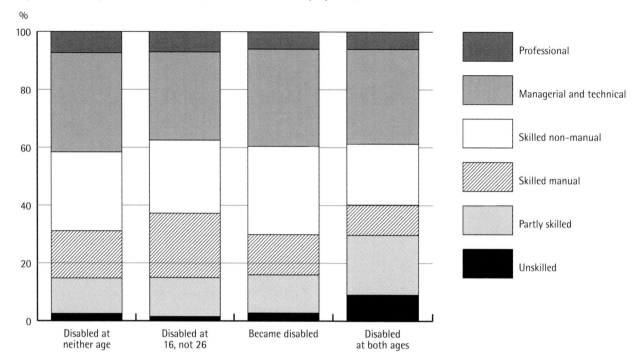

Source: BCS70 age 26 survey

At this point it may be worth pausing to consider whether it is justifiable to rank occupations in this way. If someone wanted work in a car showroom, and they succeeded in doing so, is that not an equally good outcome as for someone who wanted to become a doctor becoming a doctor? In one sense, of course, that is perfectly true, and some of the analysis here takes that approach, examining whether aspirations were or were not met. On the other hand, thinking about occupational outcomes in their own right, there are a number of ways in which a professional occupation, for example, offers more than an unskilled manual occupation. The most obvious is in terms of remuneration: the wage/salary, accrual of pension entitlements, and, often, other fringe benefits as v l. A second advantage is the degree of aut nomy associated with the work, which has consistently been found to be greater among higher-status occupations than among lower occupations. Third, the range of opportunity open to someone in a high-skilled occupation is generally greater than for someone in a lower-skilled occupation: it is easier for a doctor to become a car salesperson than vice versa. Although one might very well wish to reorganise society radically, so that lower-skilled occupations were not associated with low pay, poor conditions and limited opportunity, as things stand, these are, alas, the correlates of

low-skill occupations and it therefore makes sense to acknowledge this hierarchy of occupations in our analysis.

Earnings

Some information is also available about the hourly pay received by those in work (Table 5.2). The average (mean) rate of pay for young people disabled at neither age is £5.50 per hour, compared to £4.70 for young people disabled at both ages. A simple regression controlling for their educational qualifications indicates that disabled young people earn 11% less than non-disabled (significant at 95% level).[27]

Being out of work

Five percent of people disabled at both ages 16 and 26 have never had a paid job at all, compared to less than half a per cent of those who were disabled at neither age. This difference is statistically significant at the 99% level.

This cohort were aged 16 in 1986, a time of high youth unemployment. Over half of all groups

---

[27] Ordinary Least Squares regression on log of hourly wages

Table 5.2: Average net pay[a]

	Disabled at neither age	Disabled at 16, not 26	Became disabled between ages 16 and 26	Disabled at both ages
Hourly £	5.50	5.86	5.08[*]	4.70[**]
Weekly £	204	213	195[**]	180[**]
Number of respondents	3,439	194	576	72

Notes:

[a] Figures in 1996 prices.

Difference between 'disabled at neither age' and this group statistically significant at *90% level, **95% level.

Source: BCS70 age 26 survey

Figure 5.4: Longest period of unemployment (among those with some experience of unemployment)

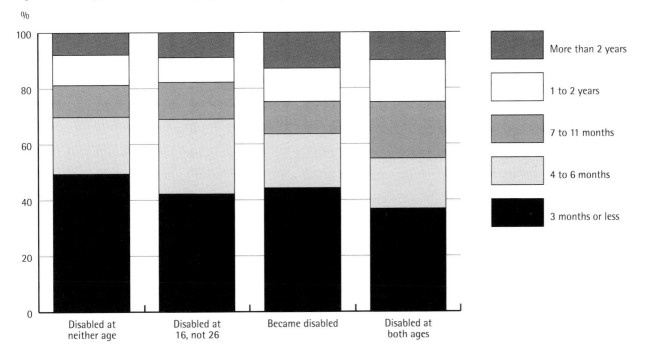

Source: BCS70 age 26 survey

experienced periods out of work: 57% of people disabled at both ages have some experience of unemployment lasting a month or more, as do 53% of people who were disabled at neither age (the difference is not statistically significant).[28] The longest single period of unemployment tends to be longer for disabled people than for non-disabled people.

Among those who have some experience of unemployment, nearly half of those who were disabled at neither age were unemployed for three months or less in a single spell, while that is the experience of only about one third of those who were disabled at both ages (Figure 5.4). At the other end of the spectrum, long-term unemployment is often classified as over six months: 30% of those disabled at neither age were ever long-term unemployed, compared to 45% of those disabled at both ages.

[28] Unemployment is a subset of being out of work. Disabled people out of work are less likely to classify themselves as unemployed than non-disabled people; hence the figures for unemployment are likely to show smaller differences between groups than figures for being out of work. However, information on duration out of work is not available in the age 26 survey.

Subjective well-being at age 26

Table 5.3 presents various indicators of how young people are feeling about their lives by the age of 26. On average, young people disabled at

Table 5.3: Subjective outlook[a]

Indicators	Disabled at neither age	Disabled at 16, not 26	Became disabled between ages 16 and 26	Disabled at both ages
(1) Self-rated labour market skills (mean score)[a]	23.7	23.4	23.7	22.5***
(2) Satisfaction with life overall (mean score)[b]	7.4	7.2*	6.8***	6.5***
(3) Malaise score (mean score)[c]	3.4	3.3	5.2***	4.6***
(4) Control over my life (% disagree)[d]	5.0	6.5	8.1***	16.2***
Number of respondents	*4,459*	*263*	*819*	*111*

Notes:

[a] Score of 1 to 4 on each of 8 skills: writing clearly, using tools properly, typing or using a computer keyboard, using a computer to solve problems or get information, looking after people who need care, teaching or instructing children or adults, carrying out mathematical calculations, and understanding finance and accounts. Higher score indicates more skills.

[b] Scale of 0 (dissatisfied) to 10 (satisfied).

[c] Score of 0 to 24; higher score indicates greater likelihood of depression and anxiety. See Rodgers et al (1999).

[d] Choice between two statements: 'I usually have a free choice and control over my life' and 'Whatever I do has no real effect on what happens to me'.

Difference between 'disabled at neither age' and this group statistically significant at *90% level, **95% level, ***99% level.

Source: BCS70 age 26 survey

both ages are less likely to feel that they have acquired skills that will be useful in the labour market than those who were disabled at neither age, and they are also less satisfied with their lives overall, and have higher average 'malaise' scores.[29] Interestingly, those who have become disabled between the ages of 16 and 26 suffer greater malaise than those who have been disabled from an earlier age, perhaps because the former are still adjusting to their new status. These differences are all statistically significant, although in some cases the magnitude of the difference is not large.

Row 4 of the table reports an interesting question about the degree of autonomy respondents feel they have. More than three times as many young people disabled at both ages, compared to those disabled at neither age, felt that 'Whatever I do has no real effect on what happens to me' more closely reflected their attitude than 'I usually have a free choice and control over my life'.

Occupational aspirations and outcomes

Figure 5.5 shows the relationship between occupational aspirations and outcomes at age 26. In general, those who aspired to professional and associate professional occupations were more likely to achieve them than those who aspired to lower-skilled jobs. Conversely, those whose aspirations were for low-status occupations such as personal and protective services, sales, and machine operatives, were more likely than other groups to be out of work at age 26.

Young people disabled at both ages 16 and 26 with the highest aspirations are less likely than their non-disabled counterparts to achieve their aspirations, but those with slightly more modest aspirations (in this case, for clerical and related or craft occupations), were more likely than other groups to exceed their aspirations. On the other hand, this group were less likely than their non-disabled counterparts to attain clerical and related or craft occupations, so that overall, they were less likely to meet or exceed their aspirations.

As we saw above, those who became disabled between the ages of 16 and 26 and those who were disabled at both ages are very likely to be out of work at age 26. This holds across all aspiration sub-groups, but is more pronounced in the lower-aspiration groups.

A majority of all groups have not attained the level of occupation that they expected when asked 10 years previously. This is partly because overall 35% expected to be working in a profession, whereas in the event only 6% are

---

[29] The malaise inventory was designed to assess mental illness (see Rutter et al, 1970).

Figure 5.5: Occupation at age 26 by aspiration at age 16

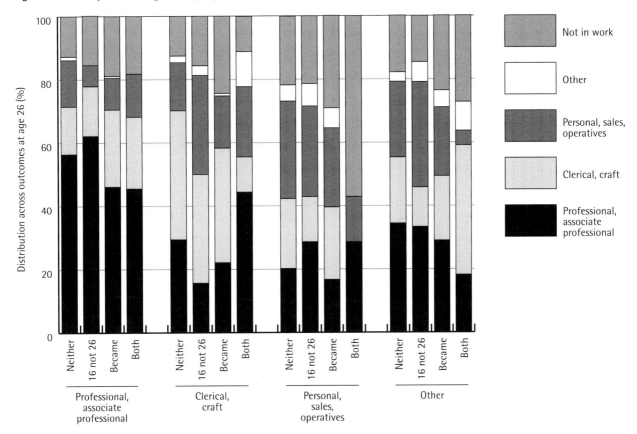

Disability status, and occupational aspiration at age 16

Source: BCS70 age 16 and age 26 surveys

doing so. Overall, 39% of young people disabled at both ages fell below their initial aspirations, compared to 28% of non-disabled young people.

Table 5.4 analyses occupational outcomes relative to aspirations, controlling for other characteristics. As was the case for the analysis of education in the previous chapter (Table 4.5), being disabled at both ages, or becoming disabled between the ages of 16 and 26 are found to be independently associated with worse occupational outcomes, controlling for aspirations, their own educational achievement and their parental background. One important implication is that a disabled young person with the same qualifications as a non-disabled young person is less likely to be in a high-status occupation. Given that their aspirations at age 16 were similar, as we saw previously, this means that young disabled people are less likely to be able to fulfil their earlier hopes.

Further analysis, testing for differential effects of parental social class on occupational outcomes by disability status, differential effects of

educational qualifications by disability status, or differential effects of aspirations by disability status, did not reveal any consistently significant interactions.

Among disabled young people, those with mental health problems at age 26 are less likely to be in high-status occupations (controlling for other characteristics), as are those who became disabled late in childhood (ages 11-16). Incorporating other characteristics that might be thought to be relevant, for disabled and non-disabled young people together, reveals that the following are independently and significantly associated with higher occupational outcomes at age 26:

- being male;
- being from any ethnic background except Pakistani/Bangladeshi;
- being from any family type except step-parent family at age 16;
- receiving a better assessment from the teacher of academic ability at age 16.

Table 5.4: Occupational attainment controlling for aspirations, disability status, own educational qualifications and parental background[a]

	Coefficient	Significance[b]
Aspiration at 16:		
Professional	Reference	
Managerial and technical	−0.257	**
Skilled non-manual	−0.124	ns
Skilled manual	−0.531	***
Semi-skilled	−0.591	***
Disability status:		
Disabled at neither age	Reference	
Recovered	−0.070	ns
Became disabled	−0.375	***
Disabled at both ages	−0.493	**
Own educational qualifications:		
Degree+/NVQ 5,6	Reference	
Higher qualification/NVQ 4	−0.626	***
A level/NVQ 3	−0.920	***
O level/NVQ 2	−1.463	***
CSE 2-5/NVQ 1	−1.919	***
None	−2.656	***
Parental social class:		
I, II	Reference	
Mixed I, II	−0.068	ns
III	−0.311	***
Mixed III	−0.426	***
IV, V	−0.671	***
Other	−0.424	***
Number of respondents	3,053	
Percentage of cases correctly classified by regression model	35.9	

Notes:

[a] Outcome ranked from 1 (out of work) to 7 (professional), so negative coefficient means this characteristic is associated with lower occupational outcome, compared to reference category.

[b] Significance: ns = not significant; * = 90%; ** = 95%; *** = 99% or higher.

Source: BCS70 age 16 and age 26 surveys

The fact that young people from Pakistani and Bangladeshi backgrounds have worse occupational outcomes is particularly striking given that, in terms of educational outcomes, they outperform young people from other ethnic groups but otherwise similar backgrounds.

Frustration and disappointment

Changes in the subjective indicators of well-being collected in the surveys at ages 16 and 26 tell us something about the way in which young people are responding to their circumstances and new experiences (Table 5.5).

Questions are asked in both surveys about the skills that the young person feels they can bring to the labour market. At both age 16 and age 26, those who are (or will turn out to be) disabled at both ages are less confident, and the gap between their assessment and that of their non-disabled counterparts (those disabled at neither age) widens over time. In other words, the experience of early adult life has taught the disabled group to down-grade their assessment of their skills, relative to the non-disabled group. Unemployment and lack of fulfilment of occupational ambitions has blunted the confidence of young disabled people.

Table 5.5: Subjective indicators of confidence and well-being[a]

	Disabled at neither age	Disabled at both ages	Difference[b]
Self-assessed skills (standardised score)			
Age 16	0.02	−0.13	0.15 ns
Age 26	0.03	−0.23	0.26 ***
Malaise (standardised score)			
Age 16	−0.01	0.14	0.15 ns
Age 26	−0.13	0.24	0.37 ***

Notes:

[a] Scores are standardised to ensure comparability between scales in different years. A higher skills score indicates greater confidence. A higher malaise score indicates lower mental well-being.

[b] Significance: ns – not significant; * = 90%; ** = 95%; *** = 99% or higher.

Source: BCS70 age 16 and 26 surveys

Sets of questions designed to assess mental well-being (the malaise inventory) are asked at both age 16 and 26. As is the case for the questions on skills, at both ages the disabled group have a higher average malaise score than the non-disabled group, and again we observe that the gap widens. This suggests that the subjective well-being of the disabled young people has deteriorated relative to their non-disabled counterparts in early adulthood.

Finally, we can compare measures of the extent to which young people feel they have control over their lives.

- At age 16, there was no significant difference in the 'locus of control' score between the non-disabled (ie those who turned out to be disabled at neither age 16 nor 26), and those who turned out to be disabled at both ages.
- By age 26, as reported above, young people disabled at both ages were more than three times as likely as those who were disabled at neither age to agree that 'Whatever I do has no real effect on what happens to me'.

This is a stark illustration of the effect that frustrated aspirations can have. Teenagers who set out with a belief that, for example, 'planning ahead can make things turn out well' have come to believe by their mid-twenties that their control over their own fate is limited.

Summary

This chapter has explored occupational outcomes at the ages of 18/19 and 26, and their relationship to earlier aspirations. The main findings are:

- There is considerable variation in the experience of the transition to early adulthood among both disabled and non-disabled young people.

- Already by the age of 18/19, and still at the age of 26, disabled young adults are less likely to be in paid work or have experience of paid work.

- Those who are in paid work have similar occupations to their non-disabled counterparts but lower pay at age 18/19; by age 26, they are disproportionately in lower-status occupations and have lower pay (even after controlling for educational qualifications).

- Those with mental health problems, more severe impairments, or who became disabled later in childhood, are at greater risk of low occupational attainment.

- Controlling for their own educational qualifications, and other background characteristics, young people who become disabled between the ages of 16 and 26, and those who are disabled at both ages, have lower occupational attainment relative to their aspirations than do their non-disabled counterparts.

- The impact of disappointment and frustrated ambition in early adulthood is apparent in the divergence between disabled and non-disabled young people's confidence, mental well-being, and sense of autonomy.

6

Transforming opportunity

This report has sought to explore the educational and occupational aspirations of young people with physical or sensory impairments, or mental health problems, in comparison to those of their non-disabled contemporaries. It has examined the way in which aspirations are, or are not, translated into educational qualifications and employment in early adulthood.

Frustrated ambition

The evidence presented in this report tells a story of frustrated ambition.

Chapter 2 showed that disabled and non-disabled young people had a similar scope and level of aspiration to remain in education, achieve qualifications, and move into high-status occupations. Around three fifths of each group want to stay on in education after the age of 16 (Table 2.1). Between a quarter and a third of each group aspire to professional occupations (Figure 2.1).

Chapter 3 confirmed these results, subjecting them to multivariate analysis. It identified four sub-groups among disabled young people who may be at risk of low aspirations:

- young people with mental health problems;
- young people with severe or complex impairments;
- young people who become disabled later in childhood (for example, during secondary school);
- young people with non-disability-related characteristics that are associated with low aspirations, such as low parental education.

Parental aspirations, education and social class are very important influences on young people (for better or worse). For example, young people with parents neither of whom have any educational qualifications are more than four times as likely to intend to leave education at 16 than young people who have at least one parent educated to degree level. There was some evidence (although not conclusive) that these influences were more important for disabled than for non-disabled young people, providing some support for the hypothesis in the literature that parents play a pivotal role in the transitions disabled young people make. Those parents who lack educational, social or material resources may need additional support, in order to promote a successful transition for their son or daughter.

The motivation and outlook of the young person him/herself was also shown to be an important determinant of aspirations. There is a stronger association here for disabled than for non-disabled young people, emphasising the importance of ensuring that disabled youngsters are encouraged to make decisions about their lives and develop self-esteem from an early age.

The analysis in Chapters 4 and 5 found that already by age 18/19, and even more so by age 26, the educational and employment outcomes for disabled and non-disabled young adults have diverged. Disabled young adults have:

- lower qualifications (Tables 4.2 and 4.4);
- higher rates and durations of unemployment (Figure 4.1, Table 5.1);
- lower pay (even after controlling for educational qualifications (Figure 5.1, Table 5.2); and
- lower-status occupations (by age 26; see discussion of Figure 5.3).

In general, educational qualifications have become a more important determinant of employment chances and occupational attainment (Bynner, 1998; Bynner et al, 2002), so under-achievement among disabled young people now carries a higher penalty than it did in the past.

The findings confirmed that aspirations are an important influence on occupational outcomes but showed that differences in aspirations could not explain the observed differences in outcomes for disabled and non-disabled young people. Their aspirations as teenagers were similar, their outcomes in early adulthood diverge. Multivariate analysis indicated that disability (either becoming disabled between the ages of 16 and 26 or being disabled throughout) was independently associated with low educational and occupational attainment, relative to aspirations. There is a presumption that this disadvantage is a result of direct or indirect discrimination, since many of the other factors that might be thought to explain the difference have been controlled for in the analysis, but the exact mechanisms are not easy to identify with this approach and discrimination remains the undifferentiated 'residual' after other plausible factors have been taken into account.

The impact of disappointment and frustrated ambition is apparent in the widening gap that opens up as young people get older, between disabled and non-disabled people's confidence, mental well-being, and belief in their ability to control their own fate.

There are encouraging and discouraging sides to these results. The encouraging aspect is that, as far as we can tell, the aspirations of disabled and non-disabled teenagers have converged since the 1970s. Walker's research on a cohort of young people aged 16 in 1974 (Walker, 1982) found that physically disabled young people were much less likely to aspire to professional and other high-status occupations. By contrast, among the cohorts studied in this research, who were aged 16 in 1986 and in 1998/2000 respectively, occupational aspirations among disabled and non-disabled young people were similar. We can speculate that this convergence has come about through a higher proportion of disabled children being educated in mainstream schools, through comprehensive education in general, or indeed through more positive role models of disabled people in society at large. In any case, the raising of disabled young people's aspirations is surely to be welcomed.

The discouraging aspect of these results is that high aspirations with relatively low chances of fulfilment are arguably the worst possible combination. As is demonstrated by the widening gap in indicators of subjective well-being between disabled and non-disabled people in early adulthood, the impact of experiencing insuperable obstacles in pursuit of one's life objectives is considerable, perhaps particularly so when the obstacles are based on direct or indirect discrimination.

In that sense, high aspirations and low chances of achievement may be worse than low aspirations and low achievement, in which case young people are denied opportunity, but they do not suffer such demoralising disappointment and intense frustration. With low aspirations and high achievement, many young people would be pleasantly surprised. High aspirations and high achievement would of course be better still.

Gaps in existing policy

This study takes place in a context of considerable policy interest in the performance of young people in education. Curriculum reform is an on-going project, aiming to boost the achievement of all young people and disadvantaged groups in particular. For further and higher education, widening participation to traditionally under-represented groups is seen as an increasingly high priority, if targets for raising overall participation are to be met.

Considerable attention is also being devoted to the situation of disabled people in the labour market. The New Deal for Disabled People (NDDP), Pathways to Work pilots, and the reform of Incapacity Benefit have all been promoted vigorously by the Department for Work and Pensions, backed by the Treasury, and the recent Cabinet Office (2005) report takes employment as one of four key areas.

It is unfortunate that these two agendas are rarely joined up. The majority of disabled people in the labour market are older people who have become disabled during the course of working life, so programmes targeted at 'return to work' for disabled people are unlikely to address the needs of disabled school leavers. The majority of New Deal for Young People participants are not dealing with problems relating to impairment or disability discrimination, so the best disabled young people can hope for from that source is diversion to Incapacity Benefit or referral to NDDP. On the other hand, under-achievement in education is seen mainly in terms of truancy, specific ethnic/gender groups such as Black Caribbean boys, and lack of basic literacy and numeracy skills – all of which are relevant to some disabled young people, but which do not identify the barriers faced by this group specifically.

New directions

Better-targeted advice and encouragement to form positive educational and occupational aspirations may be required for some specific groups among disabled teenagers: those with mental health problems, more complex needs, or who become disabled later in childhood, were identified above as being at risk of low aspirations. In addition, this study has not looked at those with learning difficulties, many of whom may need encouragement to formulate their own independent aspirations.

However, the main effort must focus on transforming the actual opportunities available to disabled young people. This study has shown that poor outcomes in early adulthood are not the result of a poverty of aspiration, so further advice and encouragement for young people are not primarily the way forward. Person-centred planning can sometimes be misinterpreted as focusing on changing the person, when attention really needs to be directed towards dismantling the obstacles to the achievement of the young person's own objectives. The following emerge as areas of concern.

- The transition from school to further education remains problematic. This was highlighted by interviewees, and confirmed by the analysis, which showed even those who expressed at age 16 an intention to stay on did not always succeed in doing so. Continuity of support, including funding, equipment and personnel, may be an important part of the solution.

- Support for entry to employment should start from the aspirations of the young person and not automatically downgrade to what is seen to be 'realistic' given their impairment. A study of young people in a disadvantaged area of

Scotland found that the unemployed rarely lacked the determination to find work but that training schemes they were sent on were often totally unrelated to their interests or intended direction, with the result that motivation was low (Furlong et al, 2003). This is too often the case for disabled young people as well, as illustrated in the interviews and case studies.

- The NDDP and the Pathways to Work initiative are both supply-side measures designed to provide incentives and advice for disabled people to move into employment. But motivation is not lacking, in general, among disabled young people leaving education, so for this group these programmes are misdirected. Work placements, combined with extending the availability of Access to Work to cover work experience, might prove to be a more effective approach.

- The other side of the coin is engagement with employers (not just advice and information as recommended by the Cabinet Office report, 2005). A New Deal for Employers could require attendance of key decision makers in companies and organisations at a Disability-Focused Interview, with tax relief from government dependent on participants signing up to an action plan to increase the employment of disabled people in their firm or organisation.[30]

- Disabled young people leave full-time education with lower qualifications than their non-disabled counterparts. There is therefore a need for more opportunities for disabled people to return to education, with maintenance or benefit payments to support the individual while studying. This is not just at the level of basic skills, but secondary and further qualifications, to improve access to higher-quality jobs. Without opportunities of this kind, the human capital that disabled young people bring to the labour market will always put them at a disadvantage.

- Serious attention should be given to the question of equal pay. This study is in line with other recent research, which has found significant gaps between the earnings of

---

[30] A similar idea was suggested by Steve Winyard of the Royal National Institute for the Blind, in response to the 2002 DWP Green Paper *Pathways to work*.

disabled and non-disabled employees, controlling for differences in occupation and educational qualifications (Burchardt, 2000). It is hard to demonstrate conclusively that these differences are the result of discrimination on the part of employers but the results are sufficiently stark to merit urgent investigation. The Disability Rights Commission could play an important role here in seeking to prosecute high-profile cases where discrimination in pay seems likely.

- The associations between parental background and educational and occupational outcomes of young people are among the strongest documented in this study. In so far as parental background is an even more significant determinant of outcomes for disabled youngsters, growing social class inequality can only serve to re-enforce the divergence in the life chances of disabled and non-disabled in early adulthood. The prospects for disabled people therefore cannot be separated from wider issues of inequality in society, and the worrying trends towards increasing strength of association between social class and educational attainment (Bynner et al, 2002).

It has been a struggle for young disabled people to gain recognition of their potential and to develop positive aspirations for playing useful roles in adult life. That achievement is certainly to be celebrated. But the fact that equality of opportunity in turning those aspirations into reality is still far from realised leaves no room for complacency. The battle is won but the war goes on.

Appendix: Definitions of disability

Youth Cohort Studies

The question asked in all recent YCS surveys is as follows:

> Do you have any health problems or disabilities, that you expect to last for more than a year, which affect your ability to carry out normal day to day activities?

Any single question is of course limited in the information it provides and it does not allow us, for example, to distinguish between those with and without cognitive impairments. However, the question is useful for comparative purposes in so far as it approximates to the 1995 Disability Discrimination Act definition of disability. It is used for all the analysis of the YCS in this report.

1970 British Cohort Study (BCS70)

There is no single definition of disability in the BCS70 age 16 and age 26 surveys. For the purposes of this study a definition has been constructed using as wide a range of information as possible and minimising the number of respondents for whom disability status is 'missing'.

At age 16, parents of the teenager in the cohort were asked:

> Does your teenager have an impairment, a disability or a handicap?
>
> (By 'impairment' we mean a physical or mental abnormality or illness. By 'disability' we mean difficulty in doing one or more mental or physical activities that average 16-year-olds can do. By 'handicap' we mean a disability which interferes with the opportunities that

others take for granted, eg problems with accessing facilities in a public building, not being considered for jobs he or she could manage if given a chance; other people are put off without even knowing what he or she is like.)

Despite the efforts of the survey designers, it appears that some parents did not fully understand the definitions being proposed, since some teenagers are reported as having a disability but not an impairment, or a handicap but not an impairment.

Health professionals (often the school nurse) administering the medical examination were asked:

> Is there any evidence that this teenager has now, or has had in the past, any significant illness, developmental problem, defect or handicap?

and

> Is there any evidence of any impairment, disability or handicap?

For each condition or impairment identified by the health professional, he or she is also asked to report whether this results in no disability, slight disability or marked disability.

The overlap between parents' and health professionals' assessments of the teenager's disability status is far from perfect. For the purposes of this report, in order to include as much information as possible, a teenager is classified as disabled:

- if he or she is identified as impaired, disabled or handicapped by the parent and as having a slight or marked disability by the nurse;

- if he or she is identified as impaired, disabled or handicapped by the parent but information from the nurse is missing;
- if he or she is identified as having a slight or marked disability by the nurse but information from the parent is missing.

If information is supplied by both parent and nurse but the information is inconsistent, the disability status of the teenage is classified as 'uncertain'. It is likely that the young people in this category have a less severe impairment, although there could be cases where the parent or nurse is aware of an impairment that is hidden to the other.

In all other cases where information is supplied by one or both of the parent and nurse, the disability status is 'non-disabled'. Where information is missing from both parent and nurse, the disability status is missing.

This approach allows us to include cases where information is available from only one source, but does not give priority to the information supplied by either nurse or parent in cases where there is disagreement. The breakdown is shown in Table A1.

For much of the analysis, this group is further restricted to those who are not reported to have learning difficulties. As explained in Chapter 1, this is not to imply that the experiences of young people with learning impairments are less important or worthy of analysis, it is simply that they are not the focus of this study. Learning difficulties are reported in a number of different ways (Table A2); the terminology is dated but reflects concepts in use at the time.

There is considerable overlap between the young people identified in these different ways. Overall, 5.8% of 16-year-olds are identified as having learning difficulties (some of whom are not disabled according to the definition above). Excluding those who are identified as having learning difficulties from the sample leaves 215 individuals who are disabled, 419 whose disability status is uncertain, and 8,668 individuals who are not disabled. The disabled thus make up 2.3% of the valid sample without learning difficulties. Cell sizes for specific analyses are sometimes lower than this because of other missing information.

Table A1: BCS70 age 16 definition of disability

	Number	%	% of non-missing
Non-disabled	8,885	76.5	91.7
Disabled	313	2.7	3.2
Uncertain	486	4.2	5.0
Missing	1,931	16.7	0
Total	11,615	100.0	100.0

Table A2: BCS70 age 16 learning difficulties

	% of valid responses
Information from parents:	
Whether dyslexic	1.7
Information from teachers:	
Whether dyslexic	0.3
Reading ability 'severely' or 'moderately impaired, relative to others of the same age	4.6
Writing ability 'well below average'	2.1
Information from nurse:	
Any mental or educational retardation	2.2
Any mental handicap	1.3

Table A3: Do you suffer from any long-term health problem, long-standing illness, infirmity or disability of any kind?

	%	Number
Yes	16.4	1,390
No	83.6	7,066
Missing		547

At age 26, the indicator is based on information from the cohort member him/herself (Table A3).

This information is compared to the classification of disability status at age 16, to construct a longitudinal indicator of disability. Where disability status is missing at either age 16 or age 26 but supplementary information (for example on specific conditions) is provided, I have used this additional information to make a judgement about the likely disability status of the individual. The breakdown is given in Table A4.

The 'Summary' column of Table A4 offers a shorter classification, allocating the 'probably' categories to their definite counterparts, and showing the percentage each category makes up of the total valid responses (ie omitting 'missing/

Table A4: Longitudinal disability status in BCS70

Disability status	Full		Summary		Summary excluding those with learning difficulties	
	N	%	N	%	N	%
Disabled at neither age	4,489	62.8	4,489	78.4	4,459	78.9
Disabled at 16, not at 26	68	1.0	279	4.9	263	4.7
Disabled at 16, not at 26 (probably)	211	3.0				
Became disabled between age 16 and 26 (probably)	40	0.6				
Became disabled between age 16 and 26	789	11.0	829	14.5	819	14.5
Disabled at both ages (probably)	48	0.7				
Disabled at both ages	81	1.1	129	2.3	111	2.0
Missing/don't know	1,418	19.9				
All	*7,144*	*100.0*	*5,726*	*100.0*	*5,652*	*100.0*

don't know'). Finally, the right-hand column of the table gives the same summary, but excluding young people who reported learning difficulties at either age 16 or 26.

Attrition from the sample between ages 16 and 26 is analysed in Despotidou and Shepherd (2002). As far as disability is concerned, 63% of those who are 'definitely not' disabled at age 16 are also respondents to the age 26 survey, compared to 61% of those who are 'definitely' disabled or whose disability status is uncertain. Those with learning difficulties or with mental health problems at age 16 are more likely than

those with other kinds of impairment to be lost to the survey. Those whose impairment is assessed by the nurse as 'marked' at age 16 are less likely to respond to the age 26 survey than those whose impairment is 'slight' or 'not disabling'. Similarly, those who attended special school are less likely to be retained in the survey than those who attended mainstream school.

Documentation for BCS70 can be found via the website of the Centre for Longitudinal Studies at the Institute of Education in London: www.cls.ioe.ac.uk/ .

References

Anderson, E. and Clarke, L. (1982) *Disability in adolescence*, London: Methuen.

Ashworth, K., Hardman, J., Hartfree, Y., Maguire, S., Middleton, S., Smith, D., Dearden, L., Emmerson, C., Frayne, C. and Meghir, C. (2002) *Education Maintenance Allowance: The first two years: A quantitative evaluation*, DfES Research Report RR352, Nottingham: Department for Education and Skills.

Audit Commission (2002a) *Statutory assessment and statement of SEN: In need of review?*, London: Audit Commission.

Audit Commission (2002b) *Special educational needs: A mainstream issue*, London: Audit Commission.

Banks, M., Bates, I., Breakwell, G., Bynner, J., Emler, N., Jamieson, L. and Roberts, K. (1992) *Careers and identities*, Milton Keynes: Open University Press.

Berthoud, R. (2003) *Multiple disadvantage in employment: A quantitative analysis*, York: York Publishing Services.

Bignall, T. and Butt, J. (2000) *Between ambition and achievement: Young black disabled people's views and experiences of independence and independent living*, Bristol: The Policy Press.

Burchardt, T. (2000) *Enduring economic exclusion: Disabled people, income and work*, York: York Publishing Services.

Bynner, J. (1998) 'Education and family components of identity in the transition from school to work', *International Journal of Behavioral Development*, vol 22, no 1, pp 29-53.

Bynner, J., Elias, P., McKnight, A., Pan, H. and Pierre, G. (2002) *Young people's changing routes to independence*, York: York Publishing Services.

Cabinet Office (2005) *Improving the life chances of disabled people*, London: Prime Minister's Strategy Unit.

Carter, M. (1962) *Home, school and work*, Oxford: Pergamon Press.

Clark, A. and Hirst, M. (1989) 'Disability in adulthood: ten-year follow-up of young people with disabilities', *Disability, Handicap and Society*, vol 4, no 3, pp 271-83.

Coles, B., Britton, L. and Hicks, L. (2004) *Building better connections: Interagency work and the Connexions Service*, Bristol: The Policy Press.

Connexions (2002) *Information to support Connexions partnerships in their work with young people with learning difficulties and disabilities*, Sheffield: Connexions.

Connexions (2003) *Connexions and mental health services*, London: Department for Education and Skills.

Connexions (2004) *Seven principles for inclusive transition planning: The final report of an East of England project on assessment and transition planning*, Sheffield: Connexions.

Cowen, A. (2001) *Room to move: A book for parents of young people with learning disabilities leaving home*, Brighton: Pavilion.

Dean, J. (2003) *Unaddressed: The housing aspirations of young disabled people in Scotland*, York: York Publishing Services.

Dearden, L., McIntosh, S., Myck, M. and Vignoles, A. (2002) 'The returns to academic and vocational qualifications in Britain', *Bulletin of Economic Research*, vol 54, no 93, pp 249-74.

Despotidou, S. and Shepherd, P. (2002) *1970 British Cohort Study twenty six-year follow-up: Guide to data available at the ESRC Data* Archive, London: Social Statistics Research Unit, City University.

Dewson, S., Aston, J., Bates, P., Ritchie, H. and Dyson, A. (2004) *Post-16 transitions: A longitudinal study of young people with special educational needs: Wave 2*, Research Report RR582, London: Department for Education and Skills.

DfES (Department for Education and Skills) (2003) *Every child matters*, London: DfES.

DfES (2004a) *Every child matters: Change for children*, London: DfES.

DfES (2004b) *Removing barriers to achievement: The government's strategy for SEN*, London: DfES.

DfES (2005) *14-19 education and skills*, Cm 6476, London: DfES.

DRC (Disability Rights Commission) (2003a) *Research summary: Survey of further education*, London: DRC.

DRC (2003b) *Research summary: Survey of higher education*, London: DRC.

DWP (Department for Work and Pensions) (2002) *Pathways to work*, Cm 5690, London: The Stationery Office.

DWP (2005) *Department for Work and Pensions five year strategy: Opportunity and security throughout life*, Cm 6447, London: The Stationery Office.

Ferri, E., Bynner, J. and Wadsworth, M. (2003) *Changing Britain, changing lives: Three generations at the turn of the century*, London: Institute of Education.

Fuller, M., Bradley, A. and Healey, M. (2004) 'Incorporating disabled students within an inclusive higher education environment', *Disability and Society*, vol 19, no 5, pp 455-68.

Furlong, A. (1992) *Growing up in a classless society? School to work transitions*, Edinburgh: Edinburgh University Press.

Furlong, A., Cartmel, F., Biggart, A., Sweeting, H. and West, P. (2003) *Youth transitions: Patterns of vulnerability and processes of social inclusion*, Scottish Executive: The Stationery Office.

Gray, P. (2002) 'Disability discrimination in education: a review of the literature on discrimination across the 0-19 age range, undertaken on behalf of the Disability Rights Commission', unpublished.

Gregg, P. (2001) 'The impact of youth unemployment on adult unemployment in the NCDS', *The Economic Journal*, no 111 (November), pp F626-F653.

Haller, A. and Miller, I. (1971) *The Occupational Aspiration Scale: Theory, structure and correlates*, Cambridge, MA: Schenkman.

Hendey, N. and Pascall, G. (2001) *Disability and transition to adulthood: Achieving independent living*, Brighton: Pavilion Publishing.

HESA (Higher Education Statistics Agency) (2004) 'HESA statistics on disabled students', www.hesa.ac.uk

Hills, J. (2004) *Inequality and the state*, Bristol: The Policy Press.

Hirst, M. (1987) 'Careers of young people with disabilities between ages 15 and 21 years', *Disability, Handicap and Society*, vol 2, no 1, pp 61-7.

Hirst, M. and Baldwin, S. (1994) *Unequal opportunities: Growing up disabled*, Social Policy Research Unit, London: HMSO.

Hussain, Y. (2003) 'Transitions into adulthood: disability, ethnicity and gender among British South Asians', *Disability Studies Quarterly*, vol 23, no 2, pp 100-12.

Johnson, A. (2005) 'Developing the Pathways to Work pilots', Letter dated 8 February from the Secretary of State for Work and Pensions to interested parties, unpublished.

Karagiannaki, E. (2005) *Jobcentre Plus or Minus? Exploring the performance of Jobcentre Plus for non-jobseekers*, CASE Paper 97, London: London School of Economics and Political Science.

Kelly, A. (1989) '"When i grow up I want to be ...': A longitudinal study of the development of career preferences', *British Journal of Guidance and Counselling*, vol 17, no 2, pp 179-200.

Lakey, J., Barnes, H. and Parry, J. (2001) *Getting a chance: Employment support for young people with multiple disadvantages*, York: York Publishing Services.

Lightfoot, J., Wright, S. and Sloper, P. (1999) 'Supporting pupils in mainstream school with an illness or disability: young people's views', *Child: Care, Health and Development*, vol 25, no 4, pp 267-83.

Loumidis, J., Stafford, B., Youngs, R., Green, A., Arthur, S., Legard, R., Lessof, C., Lewis, J., Walker, R., Corden, A., Thornton, P. and Sainsbury, R. (2001) *Evaluation of the New Deal for Disabled People Personal Adviser Pilot*, Department of Social Security Research Report No. 144, Leeds: Corporate Document Services.

Low, J. (1996) 'Negotiating identities, negotiating environments: an interpretation of the experiences of students with disabilities', *Disability and Society*, vol 11, no 2, pp 235-48.

McIntosh, S. (2001) 'The demand for post-compulsory education in four European countries', *Education Economics*, vol 9, no 10, pp 69-90.

Maziels, J. (1970) *Adolescent needs and the transition from school to work*, London: Athlone Press.

Meadows, P. (2001) *Lessons for employment policy*, York: Joseph Rowntree Foundation.

Mitchell, W. (1999) 'Leaving special school: the next step and future aspirations', *Disability and Society*, vol 14, no 6, pp 753-69.

Morris, J. (1999a), *'Hurtling into a void': Transition to adulthood for young people with complex health and support needs*, Brighton: Pavilion Publishing.

Morris, J. (1999b) *Move on up: Supporting young disabled people in their transition to adulthood*, London: Barnados.

Morris, J. (2002) *Moving into adulthood: Young disabled people moving into adulthood*, York: Joseph Rowntree Foundation.

Morrow, V. and Richards, M. (1996) *Transitions to adulthood: A family matter?*, York: York Publishing Services.

Norwich, B. (1997) 'Exploring the perspectives of adolescents with moderate learning difficulties on their special schooling and themselves: stigma and self-perceptions', *European Journal of Special Needs Education*, vol 12, no 1, pp 38-53.

O'Brien, M. and Jones, D. (1999) 'Children, parental employment and educational attainment: an English case study', *Cambridge Journal of Economics*, vol 23, no 5, pp 599-621.

Pascall, G. and Hendey, N. (2004) 'Disability and transition to adulthood: the politics of parenting', *Critical Social Policy*, vol 24, no 2, pp 165-86.

Pilling, D. (1990) *Escape from disadvantage*, London: Falmer.

Pilling, D. (1995) 'The employment circumstances at 23 of people with disabilities in the National Child Development Study', *Rehab Network*, Autumn, pp 7-11.

Polat, F., Kalambouka, A., Boyle, W. and Nelson, N. (2001) *Post-16 transitions of pupils with special educational needs*, London: Department for Education and Skills.

Preece, J. (1996) 'Class and disability: influences on learning expectations', *Disability and Society*, vol 11, no 2, pp 191-204.

Priestley, M. (1999) 'Discourse and identity: disabled children in mainstream high schools', in M. Corker and S. French (eds) *Disability discourse*, Buckingham: Open University Press.

Raby, L. and Walford, G. (1981) 'Job status aspirations and their determinants for middle and lower stream pupils in an urban, multi-racial comprehensive school', *British Educational Research Journal*, vol 7, no 2, pp 173-81.

Rodgers, B., Pickles, A., Power, C., Collishaw, S. and Maughan, B. (1999) 'Validity of the Malaise Inventory in general population samples', *Social Psychiatry and Psychiatric Epidemiology*, vol 34, no 6, pp 333-41

Rotter, J. (1966) 'Generalized expectancies for internal versus external control of reinforcement', *Psychological Monographs*, vol 80, no 1.

Rutter, M., Tizard, J. and Whitemore, K. (1970) *Education, health and behaviour*, London: Longman.

Schoon, I. (2001) 'Teenage job aspirations and career attainment in adulthood: a 17-year follow-up study of teenagers who aspired to become scientists, health professionals, or engineers', *International Journal of Behavioural Development*, vol 24, no 2, pp 124-32.

Schoon, I. and Parsons, S. (2002) 'Teenage aspirations for future careers and occupational outcomes', *Journal of Vocational Behavior*, vol 60, no 2, pp 262-88.

Schoon, I., Bynner, J., Joshi, H., Parsons, S., Wiggins, R. and Sacker, A. (2002) 'The influence of context, timing and duration of risk experiences for the passage from childhood to midadulthood', *Child Development*, vol 73, no 5, pp 1486-504.

SEU (Social Exclusion Unit) (2005) *Transitions: a Social Exclusion Unit report on young adults*, London: Office of the Deputy Prime Minister.

Skelton, T. and Valentine, G. (2002) 'Towards home and school inclusion for young D/deaf people: ways forward', *Youth and Policy*, vol 76, pp 15-28.

Tinklin, T., Riddell, S. and Wilson, A. (2004) *Disabled students in higher education*, Centre for Educational Sociology Paper No. 32, Edinburgh: Centre for Educational Sociology, University of Edinburgh.

Walker, A. (1982) *Unqualified and underemployed: Handicapped young people and the labour market*, London: Macmillan.

Watts, A., Super, D. and Kidd, J. (eds) (1981) *Career development in Britain*, Cambridge: Hobsons Press.

Wilson, L.-M. (2003) *Young disabled people: A survey of the views and experiences of young disabled people in Great Britain, conducted by NOP on behalf of the Disability Rights Commission*, London: Disability Rights Commission.

Working Group on 14-19 Reform (2004) *14-19 curriculum and qualifications reform: Final report of the Working Group on 14-19 Reform*, London: Department for Education and Skills.